GEORGE ERRINGTON

GEORGE ERRINGTON

A Test Pilot's Story

MIKE PHIPP

AMBERLEY

First published 2020

Amberley Publishing
The Hill, Stroud
Gloucestershire, GL5 4EP

www.amberley-books.com

British Library Cataloguing in Publication Data.
A catalogue record for this book is available from the British Library.

ISBN 978 1 4456 9522 8 (print)
ISBN 978 1 4456 9523 5 (ebook)

Typeset in 10pt on 13pt Sabon.
Origination by Amberley Publishing.
Printed in the UK.

Contents

Foreword

The fragmented childhood memories I have of my father were of him either under the bonnet of a sports car or indulging one of his other passions – gardening. I knew even less about what he did for a job – something to do with flying – except that it seemed to take him away for weeks and sometimes months at a time.

About the only recollection I have of this side of his life was being made to sit alongside a taxiway among some enormous aircraft for what seemed like hours, while my father talked about incomprehensible things with a lot of men in boiler suits – just how could aeroplanes 'flap', they didn't seem to be able to move their wings at all? It was extremely noisy, really rather boring and I was cold, wet and hungry. My mother later told me that my father had thought it would be a good wheeze to take me to Farnborough, where he was demonstrating that year. Without 'pilot notes' or technical manuals written about parenting, it seems that it hadn't really crossed his mind what to do with a five-year-old when he went off flying, let alone how he would keep him entertained for twelve hours whilst he talked aviation 'shop'. She was not impressed.

Despite this less than enticing introduction to his world, after his death I became increasingly intrigued by his extensive collection of aviation photographs, books, articles and notes from his engineering training in the 1920s to become a seasoned test pilot. By the time I was old enough to understand just what an extraordinary era of aviation he had lived through, however, there were few people left who could tell me about his part in it.

I was absolutely delighted when such a respected aviation author as Mike Phipp should think that my father's story was one worth researching and publishing for posterity. I gladly handed over boxes of material for him to work his magic!

Mike has crafted an extraordinary narrative about my father's life and career in aviation – the exploits, near-misses, adventures and achievements working at the leading edge of aviation technology. I can't thank him enough for bringing to life a person who I barely knew and who was involved with and accomplished so much more than I ever imagined. I hope you find the story as enthralling as I have.

I wish now that that five-year-old had shown a bit more interest on that Farnborough taxiway all those years ago.

Roly Errington
Rockford End

Acknowledgements

As mentioned in the Foreword I would not have been able to compile this book without Roly's time and assistance. Thank-you. I have gleaned further information from George's test team's notes: John Pears, Gordon Marle and Joe Tranquada. Further thanks for assistance and photos from Avro Heritage, FAST Museum, FoNFA, Mudeford Pictures, Ringwood History Centre and Solent Sky. Finally, thanks to my wife for again proofreading my efforts. This time she was pleased to find there was a story to read, not just technical information.

Introduction

George Errington was one of the band of British test pilots who began their flying in the 1930s, continuing throughout the Second World War to reach their heyday in the 1950s. As such, he ranks with the likes of Cunningham, Duke, Falk and Lithgow, among others. However, for some reason his story has remained untold.

When George set out on his working life in engineering, he had not thought of becoming a pilot, let alone a famous test pilot. As he explains, he started flying almost by accident:

> The reason for my entering aviation was, without question, the high standard of engineering associated with it. Being a qualified engineer (whatever that means!) I decided to specialise in that branch. Flying was, curiously enough, incidental and another approach to the general idea. I found that the aerodynamic conundrums connected with flying were so interesting, that I seem to have kept to this side of the job longer than originally intended.

Always associated with the Ambassador airliner, George's story shows how testing was not as straightforward as might have been imagined. During his time as a test pilot, George built up an enviable reputation. With regard to some of his exploits recalled in this book, this is what one of his contemporary test pilots wrote in 1956:

> His title might well be 'Everything happens to George'. It is true to say that he has lived the full aviation life more than anyone I know. A cynic might find some of the incidents take a bit of swallowing. However, the reverse is true as George has underwritten the extraordinary situations which seem to have come his way. Nowadays flying is so stereotyped and hemmed round by all manner of regulations that I find it both refreshing and enthralling to read of those incidents about which I had previously heard only brief reference.

This book is based on George's logbooks and the magazine articles he wrote over the years. In this way much of the story is recounted in his own words. It also shows the wide variety of aircraft he flew over the years.

Chapter 1

Starting Out in Aviation

The Errington family name hails from Northumberland where, by the 1600s, they were part of the English landed gentry. Over the following centuries many Erringtons were to enter the church. Into this setting, in January 1902, George Bertram Sainsbury Errington was born at Hunsdon, Hertfordshire – his parents were Walter Alfred and Grace Mary Errington. His father had been appointed Rector of St Dunstan, Hunsdon, in 1900, the family having moved from Ringmer, Sussex, into the Rectory at Hunsdon. Completing the family was George's older brother, John Francis, and younger sister, Mary Joan. Later his father was to become a Canon, his brother a vicar, but George found his vocation elsewhere.

By 1913 George was receiving his education at Hamilton House Preparatory School in Bath. He showed an interest in aviation and heard about a pioneer aviator who was trying to fly a homemade glider from a nearby hill. George went along to watch, recalling the man trying to launch the glider by running downhill. The glider then had to be carried back up the hill – here George's youth came to the fore. He suggested that in exchange for his help he could be given a flight by sitting on the aviator's shoulders. However, he recalled that 'its glide path somewhat resembled that of a tombstone thrown off the top of the Eiffel Tower'. There was also a French pilot visiting the Bath area. Flights were available but George could only stand and wonder at 'the bamboo machine, its mahogany propeller and the engine attached to it'. During the First World War, there was an aerial visit to the Glebe field adjoining the vicarage by a cousin who was in the Royal Flying Corps. He visited again later in the war, giving George his first flight in an Avro 504K. However, at this stage George did not envisage spending his life in aviation.

Later George attended Uppingham School at Oakham, Rutland, from where he gained entry to Sheffield University in 1920. This was in conjunction with the town's Vickers Steel Works, where he gained experience of heavy industrial engineering in their gun and armour plate works. Having served his apprenticeship and attained his university degree in 1923, George continued to work for Vickers, spending four years in their Drawing Office. In 1927, Vickers merged with Armstrong Whitworth, leading to the formation of Vickers-Armstrongs. The following year George sought a change and moved north to work for Ferranti Ltd at Oldham. Starting in the electrical engineers drawing office, he progressed to be in charge of one of their experimental departments. Whilst there, he was allowed to fly in a Gipsy Moth that was equipped with an early form of Narrow Beam Wireless which was being developed by Vincent de Ferranti and Dr R. C. Galletti – an Italian professor working for the company. Ferranti's resident pilot often took George as passenger south to Reading, where a tower had been erected in connection with the wireless trials. As a qualified mechanical engineer George realised that aviation could provide him with a higher standard of engineering. Again, he felt it was time for another change of direction from heavy to light engineering.

It was late 1929 when George made the transfer to aviation by becoming an aeronautical engineering apprentice with A. V. Roe at Newton Heath, Manchester. Here he learnt fabric sewing and woodwork before becoming a chippie and rigger on the Avro 504 and Avro Five final assembly lines. He was involved in the building of the final Avro 504Ls for the RAF, in 1931. As well as his daytime work, he undertook an evening course at Manchester Technical College, where he passed out with top honours. At this time, George considered flying was incidental to aeronautical engineering but found that the conundrums connected with flying were so interesting that he kept to that side of work longer than intended. George moved to Avro's Materials Testing Department, which involved checking fabric, wood and metal methods of aircraft construction. Avro undertook their test flying from Woodford Aerodrome, which also housed the Lancashire Aero Club. George joined the club at the end of 1929, receiving fifteen minutes' instruction on an Avro Avian on 18 December. During the spring of 1930, he received instruction from Chief Instructor 'Gas Pipe' Hall on flying Avians. By August he had received almost nine hours' instruction, so Hall considered he was ready to go solo. George undertook one further flight on 26 August, under the watchful eye of instructor Johnnie Cantrell, who also agreed that George was ready. Cantrell got out and signalled George away for his first solo flight of five minutes. Two days later he confidently flew solo for seventy minutes. Over the following weeks George built up his hours, undertaking a flight with Hall to Stag Lane on 2 October in a DH Moth. 10 October was an important date, as it was when George was issued with his Royal Aero Club of UK Aviator's Certificate No. 9550. George also studied for his A and B Ground Engineer's Licences, which he obtained in 1932.

George left Avro in 1932 due to the economic slump of the 1930s, which had resulted in the hangar staff being reduced to two. He considered joining the RAF on a Short Service Commission but was put off by an older cousin who had flown in the First World War. So, George started his own electrical engineering business, much of which involved installations in large private houses. The first of these was in North Wales and, instead of travelling by road, he decided to fly. For this he had the use of an Avian loaned to him by friend Edgar Hart. George had got to know him at Woodford, where the Avian was sitting unused in the back of a hangar. George undertook the flight to North Wales on 24 March and on 2 April was off on another job in the Peak District. From May George's base was Tedsmore Hall, near Oswestry in Shropshire, which was the home of the Revd Owen Fitzherbert Jackson – a close friend of his father.

(George's family had many connections with other families who lived in grand country houses.) The Avian operated from the Barn Field and was housed in an adjacent Dutch barn. George's engineering qualifications enabled him to maintain the Avian and his 'filling stations' were 2-gallon petrol cans. George used the aircraft as a business tool flying from A to B, frequently taking in C and D as well, with landing sites mainly being fields.

On 9 May George flew south to Shuckburgh Hall, near Daventry, the home of Sir Gerald Shuckburgh – there were strong family connections with George's grandmother being a Shuckburgh. He described his arrival:

> I circled the estate where the ancient butler was not put off by the arrival of an aeronaut. He went down to the family and announced, 'Mr Errington is overhead, m'lady'. He was quite perfect. Later the Lord of the Manor inquired 'Tell me m'boy, where did you land?'

George was impressed with the Gothic-style building and, later, the huge Christmas tree, which reached the roof of the central tower. The following day it was off to Splott in South Wales where, on landing, he was asked by the local policeman to produce his licences, although the policeman admitted he didn't know what the documents looked like. George tried to bluff him by saying it was only necessary for him to show his logbook, but then found that he had forgotten to pack it. The policeman duly reported him, and George later received a letter from the Air Ministry listing 'Documents – Aviator, the carrying of'. From Splott George flew on to Llanelli, where he had to examine some electrical equipment on a ship anchored in the bay. On arrival he found the tide was out, so he landed the Avian on a sandbank. The ship sent over a rowing boat and the job was soon completed. A crowd had gathered, no doubt hoping the tide would swamp the Avian, but George was not to be caught out and was away in plenty of time.

During 1932 George received additional instruction including aerobatics and bad weather flying. He gave an aerobatic display on 11 August at Pradoe House, near Oswestry, where a garden fete was in progress. The display was reported in the local paper:

> Flying a powerful racing Avro Avian machine, Mr Errington arrived about 5.30 and proceeded to thrill his audience with spinning nosedives, tail turns with the engine off and on, vertical loop, horizontal loops, and concluded by flying low over the grounds and returning at a fixed height which onlookers were asked to guess.

Health and Safety would have had a field day! This appears to have been the first of George's many press reports. The Avian was returned to its owner in September, with George considering his early days of private flying as a grand experience and one which taught him to heed the weather. 'May Edgar Hart know that his generosity in lending me the Avian created more true and continued happiness than perhaps he could ever have realised.'

Another airfield near Manchester was Hooton Park, where George had landed during his pilot training. It was home to Nick Comper's Comper Aircraft, which built the successful Comper Swift, a single-seat, high-performance monoplane. George was aware of their activities and visited Hooton to see their set-up. This resulted in his undertaking a thirty-minute test flight in a Swift on 27 January 1933. A few days later he flew another Swift to Tedsmore Hall and then on to nearby Oswestry. George decided to join Nick Comper and he became an Approved Inspector for the company. However, Comper was in the process of moving down to Heston in Middlesex, a move that was completed by March. George followed shortly afterwards, staying with his parents who now lived at Burleigh House, Epping. Just to the south-east of Epping was Abridge Aerodrome, which was to later prove a useful landing site for his visits home. It was from here that George was to give his mother her first flight – his father declined. George made use of his engineering skills during the final inspection of a production batch of Swifts, including undertaking some test flying for Nick. The Swift proved a very popular racing aircraft and George was assigned to oversee their Popjoy engines. In May, this included Nick's racing Swift, which was fitted with a more powerful Gipsy Major engine. It flew to Étampes-Mondésir, in France, where it competed in the Coupé de la Meurthe – a prestigious French race. During a visit home on 3 December, George was given a flight in a Bristol Fighter at Abridge, after which he was allowed forty-five minutes' solo flying. It's performance somewhat outpaced that of the Swift. On 15 December, George set off for Tedsmore Hall by Swift, but was forced to land at Shawbury due to thick fog. He continued later in the day, guided by the Wrekin mountains which protruded through the cloud layer, and ended up landing by Chirk Castle, Wrexham. He appears to have spent the Christmas holiday here, as his logbook shows that he didn't set off for Heston until 3 January.

One of the Swifts delivered from Hooton in the autumn of 1932 was *Scarlet Angel*, owned and raced by Alban Ali of Assam. In March 1933, he attempted to set a record flying between Calcutta and London. All went well until he was over Egypt, when sand clogged up the engine, resulting in a forced landing north of Cairo. The aircraft was badly damaged and abandoned by Alban Ali. Nick Comper had the aircraft shipped home to Heston for possible rebuild. As the company was in financial difficulties at the time Nick sold the wreck to George, who started its restoration in his spare time. This occupied the first half of 1934 and George described the undertaking in the *Aeroplane Magazine* as follows:

> I had the greatest longing for a private aeroplane, and had the chance to get fairly cheaply a broken Swift with the engine on the wrong side of a very necessary complete overhaul. One piece of good fortune; I was a fully licensed ground engineer, etc. – absolutely essential if expenses were to be kept down to a minimum.

> Saturday afternoons and Sundays only were available for rebuilding the aeroplane, and doing a complete overhaul of the engine. Every Sunday evening I said 'Never again', but my enthusiasm returned during the week. A calibrated 'fan' was borrowed, and a test bed was loaned by a well known aeronautical college. I put engine No 109 through the tests and all went well. The BHPs were right on the dotted line.
>
> I proudly carried the engine back to the airframe in the dickey of an old motorcar, speculating on all the wonderful flights to be. Final assembly and flow tests were OK; then came my own idea of a colour scheme, which was to be unique, and all was set for the test flight. I might add that the interim snags and moments of despair were multitudinous, but on August 4 1934, the result of six months weekend work was put to the test.
>
> Several friends stood about to witness the disaster, but she leapt off the ground as all good Comper Swifts do and the whole thing stayed together in a most estimable manner. I thought that if anything was going to burst, now was a fitting opportunity, so we rocketed up to 12,000 foot at full throttle. All went well, the engine ran perfectly, the rebuilt undercarriage stayed put on landing, and that was that – I was at last a private owner with a real home-earned Certificate of Airworthiness.

George believed that for a private aeroplane to be of any use it had to take its owner to his destination without having the aggravation of landing at airports with the associated delays. He set out to prove this with his 'new' Swift G-ACTF, which retained its *Scarlet Angel* name, recording events with his faithful Vest Pocket Kodak (VPK) camera, which he carried in the Swift's locker. In his spare time George undertook a special engine building and testing course with Armstrong Siddeley Motors, followed by a similar course with Wolseley Aero Engines at Castle Bromwich. This was to increase his aero engine licences, adding to his C, D and X Ground Engineer's Licences.

May 1934 saw George fly to France in the Desoutter I of Richard Shuttleworth (he was also Director of Comper) in order to attend the Coupé Deutsch Race at Étampes-Mondésir on 27 May. George left Heston on 23 May and flew down to Lympne to clear customs. The engine needed attention and it was dusk before he reached Le Bourget. Next day it was on to Étampes, where he met up with Nick Comper. Nick had entered his new racing plane – the Comper Streak – in the race but undercarriage problems forced him to retire. George started for home on the 28 May, but a broken engine pushrod resulted in a landing at Lympne with the aid of floodlights. George borrowed a Gipsy Moth to fly up to Heston to get the necessary parts to make repairs so as to get home. George flew down to Portsmouth on 19 July for what turned out to be an important meeting with the directors of the Airspeed company. The reason was the perilous state of Comper Aircraft, which went into liquidation in August, being taken over by the Heston Aircraft Company. There was a new board of directors and, although they took George on as an inspector and part-time pilot, he decided it was a good time to move on.

A sketch made by George's father – the Revd Walter Errington – in 1901 of St Dunstan Church, Hunsdon. The family lived in the adjacent rectory.

Right: A youthful-looking George in the 1920s.

Below: In his younger days George covered many miles by motorbike. Many of these were taken up with visits home to Hunsdon.

A view inside the vast Avro Aircraft factory at Newton Heath, Manchester, where George commenced work towards the end of 1929.

George received flying instruction on Avro Avians at Woodford Aerodrome in 1930, obtaining his pilot's licence in October.

Following a rebuild at Hooton Park, Comper Swift G-ABUA was flown by George on a visit to Tedsmore Hall early in 1933.

The new Comper Aircraft factory built at Heston, where George commenced work for Nick Comper in the spring of 1933.

Arriving by air in May 1932 at one of the stately homes George visited. This is Shuckburgh Hall near Daventry, the home of Sir Gerald Shuckburgh.

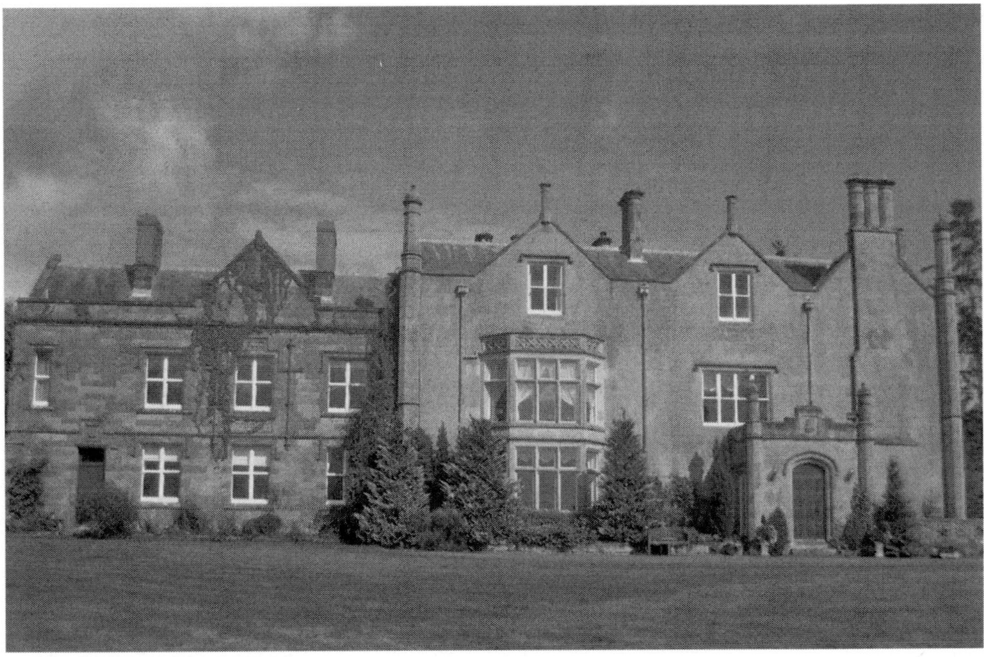

For a while during 1932 George kept Avian G-AAHK at Tedsmore Hall, Oswestry, the home of family friend Revd Owen Jackson.

Chapter 2

Early Days with Airspeed

Airspeed Ltd had been established in York in March 1931 and moved south to Portsmouth in March 1933. The company had developed the single-engined Courier, the first British airliner fitted with flaps and a retractable undercarriage. From the Courier, Airspeed developed the twin-engined Envoy, which was flown in June 1934. George had seen a Courier when it visited Heston and was impressed by its retractable undercarriage – a novelty at the time. Although only a small firm, George saw a future with Airspeed and contacted their Managing Director – Nevil Shute Norway. This resulted in George flying down to Portsmouth on 19 July, where he thought a reception had been laid on for him. His arrival coincided with a RAF display which saw the likes of Hawker Furies, Handley Page Hiniadies and Vickers Virginias parked around the airfield. Despite its small size, the Swift soon attracted the crowd's attention. George headed for the Airspeed factory where Nevil introduced him to the other Joint Managing Director, Hessell Tiltman. Another director was Sir Alan Cobham, but he was away much of the time with his Flying Circus and developing his ideas for Flight Refuelling. Nevil looked after the general management of the commercial side and sales, with Hessell looking after technical and design aspects. George seemed to hit it off with Nevil straight away, soon meeting him socially along with his wife Frances. George was offered the job of inspector on new Couriers and Envoys as from 23 September, his Ground Engineers Licences proving of great assistance and value to the company.

Prior to commencing work, George undertook a couple of weeks touring in his Swift. He later wrote an article entitled 'Sporting Flying' for the *Aeroplane*, detailing these exploits. Destinations included Woodford, Chatsworth, Tedsmore Hall, Gatwick, Overton, Christchurch, Lacock and many more. His recollection of first visiting Christchurch airfield was of two old Avro 504s dumped in a corner of the field. At the time he did not realise how important Christchurch was to become in his flying career. George recalls visiting friends at Seaton on the Devon coast:

> One Sunday we [Swift and George] were to meet friends on the Devon coast, all very hilly and difficult for parking, so we just had to land up the side of a valley. One must be more careful as there is no such thing as a muffed approach or a clamber out on the engine. The advantage of a single seater is it can be lifted by the skid and trundled about like a wheelbarrow. If space demanded I usually folded the plane and got her into a corner or behind a haystack.

Then there was a visit to neighbouring Dorset:

> Landed on the top of a hill in Milton Abbas in a field full of mushrooms, large quantities of which were put in the locker prior to take-off. In this manner one can visit many beautiful parts of the country.

A lady ran up with excitement, exclaiming, 'I watched you and was sure there was going to be an accident. But you brought the aeroplane down so gently. You must be a wonderful pilot.' George ruined her day by responding 'Oh, I'm not too bad when I'm sober.'

Airspeed had undergone a financial reorganisation in July 1934, with shipbuilders Swan Hunter becoming the major shareholder of the newly formed Airspeed Ltd (1934). This provided the company with financial stability whilst developing the Envoy and other projects. To promote their wares, Airspeed backed entries of a Courier and a Viceroy (modified Envoy) in the October 1934 England to Australia Air Race starting from Mildenhall. George joined Airspeed's Inspection Department as works number AS11 and was involved with the two air race aircraft. Another job was supposedly to fly down to Lyons where a Courier had damaged its undercarriage. He was to fly to Paris from Croydon by HP42 airliner and was told his ticket would be waiting for him at Croydon. The departure time came and went – no ticket appeared. Airspeed's funds were rather depleted at the time and so George returned home. The Courier's pilot managed to fix his undercarriage down and decided to fly back to Portsmouth. He arrived just after dusk and misjudged the landscape, landing in Langstone Harbour, just short of the airfield. Next morning, the Courier was pulled off the mudflats and into the hangars where George's engineering skills were soon put to use in its repair.

Airspeed's directors agreed that George could keep his Swift in one of the hangars at Portsmouth. He used it for business during October 1934, visiting Wolseley Aero Motors at Castle Bromwich (their engines powered a number of Envoys), and then on to Mildenhall in connection with the Australian Air Race. En route to High Post, on 18 November he stopped off at family friend Charles Waring, who lived at Moyles Court House, near Ringwood. This was to be a frequent stopping-off point over the following years. (On his marriage in 1949 George and his wife were to live in a house a short distance from Moyles Court House. However, this was still in the future.) At the time George joined Airspeed, their Chief Test Pilot was Flt Lt 'Percy' Colman. A major change in George's life occurred in May 1935. He had been happy as an inspector but, on 20 May, for some reason, Percy was not around to test fly a Courier. Knowing that he was an able pilot, Nevil offered the task to George, resulting in a fifty-five-minute test flight. What influenced events was the comprehensive report that George provided – produced from an engineer's point of view, not a pilot's. As a result, George was offered the job of test pilot in charge of experimental and development flying, which he happily accepted, although commenting 'Dogsbody pilotage duties'. A week later saw George take a Convertible Envoy on a test flight, then on 4 June he took up a Lynx-engined Envoy on his first 'official' flight in his new role as test pilot.

There were still many flights in his Swift. The end of May 1935 saw the start of frequent visits to Charborough Park, near Wimborne, and then on 23 June again up to Tedsmore Hall, where he found the grass in the Barn Field was tall:

> I set about looking for a good landing field and sighted one with sheep grazing. This meant no damage would be done to crops by landing. Sheep are very good and much more obliging than cows or horses as they move about in a platoon. The day I landed the grass was more or less up to the engine in spite of the sheep. It was custom to take off early Monday mornings in order to return to work. The friendly farmer sportingly offered to cut a runway diagonally from corner to corner, approximately into wind.

A much more demanding trip was a Scandinavian Tour which commenced on 28 July. Described as a six-day holiday, George left Portsmouth, cleared customs at Lympne and Le Zoute, before arriving at Amsterdam. On 30 July he proceeded to Hamburg and on to Copenhagen the following day. The Danish press picked up on his arrival, seeming surprised at the distance George had covered. They ran the story as follows:

> **A Fast Lilliput**
>
> The world-known English Aircraft-factory 'Airspeed's' test pilot, Mr Errington, arrived here yesterday on a flying holiday-visit, in a very amusing machine.
>
> It is a black-green Comper Swift, a single seat monoplane, and it is so small that one can almost have it standing on the desk. The engine is a 75 hp Pobjoy, air-cooled radial, and that it really is something very effective was demonstrated yesterday, when it very nicely kept pace with the Danish Airliner from Hamburg, and landed simultaneously at Kastrup, although it only started three minutes ahead at Fuhlsbüttel. And the Danish machine is doing about 220 kph.
>
> Mr Errington has a six day vacation and this small breathing space in his strenuous and dangerous life, he is using to visit Copenhagen in his small and fast, but somewhat unsociable toy – it will only hold Mr Errington himself. Its dimensions are five metres by seven, so it is really a Lilliput, the smallest machine ever seen here in Copenhagen.
>
> The starting point for Mr Errington's trip is Portsmouth, where the Airspeed factory is, and from there he has gone to Amsterdam and Hamburg and then to Copenhagen. Tomorrow he is going to Stockholm and Mr Errington may also visit Helsingfors.

From Copenhagen, George crossed to Malmo for customs clearance, and then on 2 August he flew the 330 miles to Stockholm, over vast forests and lakes, in three hours and five minutes. He stayed here for a few days, taking in the Swedish Aero Show. The Swedish press also made play of this Englishman making such a long-distance flight. George's flight out could not have been too daunting as on his 5 August return he flew a total of 777 miles in just over seven hours. This was made up of Stockholm to Malmo (three hours), on to Copenhagen (fifteen minutes) and then four hours to Amsterdam. A night's sleep saw George ready for the home leg to Lympne, Rochester, and finally Portsmouth.

George had one day off after returning from Scandinavia before he was back to work test flying. Envoys flown during the summer of 1935 included OK-BAM for CSA Czechoslovakia, Lynx-powered V16 on demonstration to Japanese officials (despite 'heavy rain and low cloud on the day') and Wolseley-powered G-ACVI, whose passengers included Nevil. Envoy G-ACVJ was demonstrated to Bata pilots at Gravesend on 13 October; the prototype Envoy was flown to Martlesham for trials on 22 October; flight instruction was given to Nevil on 25 October; Convertible Envoy V18, fitted with an upper gun turret, was tested on 16 December, then flown to Farnborough the following day with firing trials undertaken later in the month.

Despite having progressed to a test pilot, George decided he needed further flight training. He arranged to visit Air Service Training at nearby Hamble for blind flying instruction. He flew to Hamble on the afternoon of 3 January 1936 where he received his first lesson from Flt Lt Beaumont. Fifty minutes was spent flying an Avro Cadet, before returning to Portsmouth in the dark. Instruction on Cadets continued until April, including cross-country flights and spins. The Envoy prototype had been modified as the Envoy II with higher-powered Wolseley Scorpio engines and underwing split trailing edge flaps. This reduced the aircraft's landing run by half, also reducing its landing speed. Envoy V18 undertook gun stability trials in connection with an anticipated South African order. Pilot training was given to 'Herr Udet' in the Envoy prototype during the spring, including night flying instruction. 'Herr Udet', as George described him, was a mercenary pilot who intended to fly the Viceroy for Haile Selassie – the Emperor of Abyssinia. There was a civil war in progress and the aircraft was to be used as a bomber. Little conversion work had been undertaken before the Emperor was overthrown in March, so 'Herr Udet' was out of a job and the Viceroy was put up for sale. A leisurely flight on the morning of 27 March involved positioning a Courier over the Queen Mary for publicity photographs by *Flight* magazine. Percy Colman joined in by flying an Envoy with Hessell and Nevil on board as passengers. Whilst working on Couriers and Envoys during the spring, George found one of the woodworkers became very interested as to how an aircraft flew. George was happy to show him the controls and what effect they had on an aircraft's flight. He later found out the reason for the man's interest. On 20 August the worker and a colleague commandeered a brand-new Courier and, early in the morning, tried to take off with the intention of delivering the aircraft for use in the Spanish Civil War. After a number of attempts the Courier crashed on the north side of the airfield, fatally injuring one of those on board. Nevil issued a statement: 'This act was unauthorised by the Company who had no knowledge of this foolhardy attempt.' George was out of the country at the time.

George's parents moved from Epping to Ringwood in 1936, renting a substantial farmhouse to the east of the town known as 'Old Stacks'. His father was not in the best of health, probably suffering from the early stages of dementia, so George would drive over from Portsmouth whenever possible. However, in order to cut down on these journeys and save time he took lodgings in Portsmouth. He frequently used the Swift to travel home, landing in a field adjacent to Moyles Court House. Over the years George had built up a friendship with Thurstan James of the *Aeroplane* magazine. He corresponded with him and, in 1936, wrote an article on the advantages of the wing flaps used on the Envoy. This was the first of a number of items George had published over the years.

Impressed with their Courier airliner design, in the summer of 1934 George decided to join the Airspeed company at Portsmouth.

A 1934 view of the expanding Airspeed factory situated on the south-eastern side of Portsmouth Airport.

The prototype Airspeed Envoy G-ACMT on show at Portsmouth in the summer of 1935 during a visit by RAF Furies and Virginias.

George poses with the prototype Envoy G-ACMT, in 1934. It had been first flown by Percy Colman in June.

Waiting between test flights at Portsmouth, early in 1936, are Percy Colman, Frank Turner (sales manager) and George.

Above left and right: The Airspeed Managing Directors – Nevil Norway (left) and Hessell Tiltman (right). George quickly established a friendship with both.

George's 'business tool' – his Comper Swift G-ACTF – on the newly mown runway at Tedsmore Hall, 1935.

In 1936 the Errington family moved to Old Stacks – a large farmhouse on the outskirts of Ringwood.

The family at Old Stacks: George, his father, sister, mother and brother. Unfortunately, such family gatherings were infrequent.

Chapter 3

South African Adventure

During the spring of 1936 Airspeed were working on seven Envoy IIIs for South Africa. Three were for the Defence Department and four for South African Airways. The military ones were to be used as fast medium bombers, being fitted with an upper gun turret, a machine gun in the nose and underwing racks for carrying small bombs. The first for the Air Force, 251, was flown on the morning of 21 May and then frequently by George during its trials. ZS-AGA – the first for SAA – was demonstrated on the morning of 1 July, only a few days before its delivery flight was due to be commenced. The Airspeed directors had already agreed that the first two aircraft would be delivered by air, with the others following by sea. Record attempt flights to Cape Town were becoming more common, with Sir Alan Cobham recalling his survey flights in the late 1920s. George was aware of a flight by a young Victor Smith in March 1933, undertaken in the same sporting aircraft he flew – a Comper Swift. Then, at the end of May 1936, Lord Nuffield had arranged for his Envoy to be flown to Cape Town and back, so demonstrating his company's new Wolseley Scorpio engine. However, at the time manufacturers would still normally deliver aircraft by sea over such long distances. For additional publicity value, the South African Air Force would provide a crew, who arrived at Portsmouth in June for training. George 'volunteered', flying ZS-AGA along with Capt. Wilson of the SAAF, with 251 flown by two SAAF pilots. The South African Minister of Defence – Oswald Pirow – visited the factory on 17 June, arriving in a RAF Dragon Rapide. He needed to check on the plans for the delivery flight of which he was to be part.

In view of the impending African trip, George decided to sell his Swift and the deal was done at the end of June. As a swansong George flew it to Tedsmore Hall on 27 June, undertaking a final fifteen-minute flight at Portsmouth on his return. He then handed the Swift over to locally based Capt. Francis Luxmoore.

The following details of the South African flight are based on George's report. On 4 July 1936 the machines left Portsmouth for the 7,000-mile flight to Johannesburg. They flew to Cologne, Frankfurt and Vienna in foul weather, and then on to Budapest, Belgrade, Salonica and Athens. From Athens they flew to Crete where their ETA was 120 seconds out in 250 miles. At El Salloum, on the northern Egyptian coast, they were told that they had landed on the edge of one million square miles of the Arabian Dessert, where it had not rained for six years. The meteorological report suggested that it would not do so for a further sixty years, so the crews hurriedly left. The pilots were impressed with the take-off performance of the Envoy on a short runway in intense heat as they left for Cairo. From Cairo, where they were joined by two Westland Wapitis, they flew at low altitude over the Valley of the Kings and landed at Luxor among Arabs who were most interesting, and had a distinct sense of humour, in addition to distinct scents. Leaving a covey of Arabs guarding the machines, the crews were transported into town over a rather amazing road in an equally amazing car, which also had a sense of humour. The vehicle hit a large rut in the road, with the hood collapsing on top of the passengers. They left Luxor on 8 July for Khartoum, over the Blue Nile, down the White Nile and around a violent thunderstorm over the Nubian Dessert. Malakal was the first aerodrome they encountered with a runway. The wind was blowing across it, so the Envoy had to land on soft ground, quite happily as it turned out. Then over Anglo-Egyptian Sudan for a night stop in Juba, where the SAAF engineer surveyed his surroundings whilst extracting oil filters and examining tyres, propellers and the airframe. From Khartoum they flew to Nairobi, via Kisumu, to pick up Oswald Pirow, who was flying on the final leg to Pretoria. George waited for a lift in 251, which had been delayed at Cairo by RAF personnel who showed great interest in the Envoy. Mr Pirow was the first to welcome the crew on the tarmac at Pretoria. He and his party were impressed with the report of the flight given to them by Capt. Wilson. 5,000 miles had been flown in thirty and a half hours in great comfort. Four days later George boarded 251 and flew to Roberts Height, Pretoria, via Dodoma and Mbeya, where he noticed endless miles of scrub with bush fires raging in all directions. Finally, to Rand Airport, Johannesburg – a total of forty-three and a half flying hours. George ended his account with a handsome tribute to the Shell Company's organisation, 'which had 87 octane fuel waiting for them even hundreds of miles from railways, whilst four Cheetah engines behaved beautifully all the time giving never a moments anxiety'.

After a short break, George flew on board a SAA Ju52 to Wingfield Aerodrome, Cape Town, on 29 September. Here he was responsible for the erection and testing of the four Envoys that had been shipped out. ZS-AGB had been unpacked from its crate at Wingfield and flight trials were then undertaken at Johannesburg and Cape Town, later taking in the high altitude of Roberts Heights. With two aircraft available, SAA were able to open the route from Johannesburg to Port Windhoek on 9 October, and to Port Elizabeth on 12 October. On the evening of 5 November, George was overseeing a SAA pilot who was flying ZS-AGC on his first flight as captain. Despite two green lights, one of the undercarriage legs folded up on landing, with the Envoy ending up in a cloud of dust. Luckily there was little damage and the aircraft was soon back in the air. George received a few column inches in the Cape Town press, which covered his testing of the Envoys. Commenting on the long delivery flight George said, 'We were not attempting records; we simply flew at our normal cruising speed.' On his job as a test pilot, 'People think it is dangerous. I find it safer than motoring in Cape Town.'

At the same time as the Envoys were being delivered, the Schlesinger Air Race was taking place between Portsmouth and Johannesburg. Unfortunately, the race appeared fated. Some competitors withdrew before the start, nine finally set off and only one made it to Johannesburg. Most of the others crashed en route. One of the entrants was Envoy G-AENA *Gabrielle* (ominously race No. 13), which set off on 29 September. Due to poor weather it landed at Abercorn, Northern Rhodesia, on 1 October.

Abercorn was an official stopping-off point but lacked public communication with the outside world. As a further problem the area around the southern end of Lake Tanganyika was covered in smoke haze from bush fires. G-AENA's take-off was unsuccessful, with *Gabrielle* crashing and breaking up, killing two of the four crew. Airspeed were keen to assist the resultant investigation, cabling George to fly up from Johannesburg. He set off with a novice mechanic in a Puss Moth on 10 October, flying via Bulawayo, Victoria Falls, Broken Hill and Mpika. Two days later, the next sector went wrong due to a combination of factors. Bush fires continued to make visibility bad and George was unable to locate Abercorn. The aircraft's compass ring had broken, as had George's watch – throwing out his calculations. After three hours flying, he realised that he was lost:

> The situation was quite hopeless. I hadn't a clue where I was. The map of Tanganyika was useless because of lack of detail. Then I saw my petrol gauges were getting dismally low. Another mountain range loomed up, so I knew the terrain was impossible for landing. This should have been one of those occasions when at the critical moment an aerodrome turns up and all is well. There was nothing for it but a forced landing.

George put the Puss Moth down on a hillside covered in elephant grass. On leaving the aircraft he discovered the area was surrounded by ant hills and that he was lucky not to have hit one. Then the ants started crawling all over George, who had climbed onto one of the aircraft's wheels and spent his time trying to get rid of them. After a while he saw some natives, but they stayed away as they had never seen an aircraft before. At nightfall they departed back to their village, leaving George and his mechanic with the aircraft. George managed to get some sleep by 'tying his head to the cockpit roof'. Next morning the natives returned with their chief, who explained that the tribe people regarded him as God, as he had come out of the sky. The flyers were offered some bantam eggs for breakfast, but George explained that he couldn't eat them raw, so all they had for sustenance was some water which had collected on the aircraft's wings. Getting frustrated, George wrote an SOS message requesting confirmation of his whereabouts plus petrol, asking the chief to get it delivered 'to the nearest White Man'. Help eventually arrived in the shape of the local District Commissioner who, naturally, brought along a flask of tea. He also had a map and arranged for four gallons of fuel to be brought along. He explained that there was an Imperial Airways emergency landing ground a short distance away, which he didn't think had ever been used. Instructed by sign language, the natives cleared a strip through the scrub for the aircraft, which George estimated as 250 yards. Luckily it was just enough, although the wheels hit the scrub bushes at the end. It was only fifteen minutes to the landing ground, where George was able to thoroughly check over the Puss Moth. It was then only another forty-five minutes to his intended destination at Abercorn. Concern had already been raised after the Puss Moth failed to arrive and a telegram had been sent saying that George had not arrived as expected. This was reported in the *Cape Times* and *Portsmouth City News* as 'British Pilot lost in Africa'. The South Africans dispatched one of their new Envoys from Roberts Heights to take part in the search. However, on his safe arrival George was able to send a message saying, 'Everything OK.' Going back to his original task,

George reported on what he found at *Gabrielle*'s crash site, but there was little he could do. Seeing the mangled remains of the Envoy he considered it a miracle that two of the crew had escaped. He gave evidence to the local Provincial Commissioner and his report was used in the official investigation. At midday on 19 October, George started his return south, finding difficulty around Mpika and Broken Hill due to the continuing bush fires. The smoke screen proved very troublesome and at times reduced visibility to half a mile. Then, between Lusaka and Salisbury, he encountered low cloud which made flying difficult as he did not know the country. He made it back safely, taking a few days off before returning to Wingfield.

SAAF Envoy 253 had been reassembled and was test flown on 30 October, followed by ZS-AGC. Later this was test flown from Wingfield, including an instructional flight on 26 November for Capt. Bates, taking in Beaufort West and Kimberley. On 18 November George gave instruction to SAAF pilots at Roberts Heights. This completed the Envoy testing and training, but George managed a few other flights. His highlight was flying an elderly SAAF DH9 fighter at Roberts Heights on 11 December. After a quick early morning familiarisation flight with Capt. Donnelly, George undertook a twenty-five-minute solo flight – certainly one for his logbook. Due to return to England, George received a telegram asking him to assist with one of the air force's machines which had hydraulic pump problems. He borrowed a Rearwin Sportster to fly to Beaufort West and then Aliwell North on the Orange River. Here he was able to render assistance in solving the Envoy's problems. Then on to East London, Port Elizabeth, with an appropriate night stop at George, before returning to Cape Town on 16 December. He found the country he flew over magnificent, although he experienced all sorts of weather and turbulence.

This was George's last flight in South Africa as he returned home on 18 December on board Union Castle's *Edinburgh Castle*. He estimated that he flew 13,500 miles during his African adventure and considered Uganda and Cape Province the best parts. His memories were of marvellous blue skies and a grand climate. George arrived at Southampton on 4 January 1937 and, after his 'break' in Africa, returned to his normal test flying at Portsmouth. At the beginning of April, he gave flying lessons to Nevil and Alfred Townsley – a newly appointed director. For a change of aircraft, George had a quick flight in a Praga Baby, which visited Portsmouth on 3 March, and had twenty-five minutes' aerobatics in Lord Nuffield's Wolseley-powered Hawker Tomtit on 31 March, during its visit to Portsmouth.

George recorded various Envoys he was involved with at the beginning of 1937. Airspeed received an order for a VIP version to serve with the RAF King's Flight. Flown on 25 March, G-AEXX was delivered to Martlesham Heath on 21 April for trials, before being accepted by The Flight in June. George had already given flight instruction to Sqd Ldr 'Mouse' Fielden, the Flight's captain. Envoy III OK-VIT had been damaged in a crash-landing at Antwerp on 19 February, whilst en route back to Portsmouth. Brought home for repairs, it was tested by George on 14 May. A VIP Envoy for the Maharaja of Indore suffered engine vibration problems during flight trials in April, resulting in a change of its engines. This seems to have worked as it was used by George on a sales demonstration flight on 27 May.

George and the first South African Air Force Envoy 251, at Portsmouth, in May 1936, prior to it receiving its paint scheme.

Percy Colman positions South African AF Envoy 251 over the Hampshire clouds for the press. Note the gun turret on this military version.

Well into the African delivery flight sees a fuel stop on 7 July in Luxor, Sudan, for ZS-AGA of South African Airways. George is not in his usual smart attire.

A view from the cockpit of ZS-AGA as it overflies a mountainous area.

On the Envoy delivery flight to South Africa George has to record his overflying the impressive Victoria Falls.

Envoy ZS-AGB, which had been shipped out by sea, then reassembled at Wingfield and made ready for flight testing under George's supervision.

Standing proudly by the third South African Air Force machine at Wingfield, George has just overseen its final assembly.

Seen at the handover of one of the South African Airways Envoys are George, the local Airspeed agent and Capt. Robinson of SAA.

Preparing to set off in Puss Moth ZS-ADK, from Johannesburg for Abercorn, George did not realise this was going to prove such an eventful journey.

Following the forced landing in the wilds of Mzeka, George tries to organise a take-off for the Puss Moth with local help.

Chapter 4

Followed by a Chinese Adventure

In 1936 Airspeed received an order for an Envoy III from the Military Governor of Kwangsi Province, in Southern China. G-AERT was built to meet the order and was first flown by George on 14 January 1937. The Governor was happy to pay for the Envoy to be flown out, not crated and shipped. The delivery flight was undertaken by Percy Colman, with Airspeed apprentice W. Locke as 'engineer' and Nevil's wife Frances as a passenger as far as Calcutta. G-AERT departed eastwards on 27 January and, after a relatively uneventful 9,000-mile trip, reached Liu Chow, north-west of Hong Kong, on 12 February. After demonstration flights around Kwangsi, Percy cabled Airspeed to say that the Governor wanted a second Envoy. There was little publicity of Percy's epic flight, although an Airspeed advertisement noted, 'Another long-distance flight. Portsmouth to Hong Kong in 14 days.'

Whilst Percy returned home Airspeed prepared the second aircraft, G-AEXE, during April 1937, which was tested by George. As Percy had delivered the first aircraft, George was 'volunteered' (again) to deliver the second. Although ready to go, payment for the aircraft was not received until mid-June. This annoyed George as he had wanted to get away earlier, knowing that the monsoon season was about to start over the Indian sub-continent. Then one morning Nevil shouted out the office window to George, 'Off you go, I have the cheque in my hand.' G-AEXE finally got away to its first stop in Marseilles on the afternoon of 14 June. George had always been greatly interested in cloud formations and this trip was to provide him with a great variety to study. George recounted his experiences for the *Aeroplane* on his return in September:

> My Envoy went great guns – the motors ran faultlessly throughout. We personally did all scheduled inspections and maintenance, myself and student-engineer Ronnie Graham, who had the 8-seater cabin all to himself. I greatly admired his enthusiasm and appreciated his help.
>
> Portsmouth – Hong Kong in 50 hours 58 minutes was good going considering the weather conditions, and I had also to deviate to Hsiukoukwang and Pak-Hoi in SW China (Government orders), before making Hong Kong.
>
> The final flight to Liu Chow in Kwangsi province showed an average of 174 mph, using a borrowed 33 years old map. Yes it is time that China bought some men, telescopes and croquet-poles to do some surveying and to satisfy a lamentable want in Eastern Aviation.

The flight is related in greater detail from George's notes, recalling the various trials and tribulations. Marseilles was reached in three hours twenty minutes, but departure for Italy was delayed until the following afternoon, with George noting the Benito-type cumulus clouds. Rome was invisible in a rainstorm, which worsened over the Naples area, but George found the Sperry navigation equipment kept the Envoy on track. However, the storm had knocked out all radio and telegraph communications and so they arrived unannounced at Brindisi. Day three was a shortish trip to Athens, prior to crossing the Mediterranean to Cairo. George recorded their speed as 185½ mph, which he considered up to Empire flying boat standard. Day five was an early start with Basrah as the planned destination. All went well over the Holy Land, with George commenting that he considered the Dead Sea had gone all commercial at one end with its salt pans and developments. After refuelling at Rutbah Wells good progress was made with a 'real matey tail wind' increasing their speed to 206½ mph. An early departure followed for the next stage over the Persian Coast. George complained that it 'gave [him] a pain in the neck with its continuous sandstorms, heat and poor visibility'. This meant that it took some time to find their refuelling point at Task, prior to continuing to Karachi. The two crew spent the next day cleaning and servicing the Envoy, prior to flying across the top of India in one day. Dust storms were encountered most of the way to Jodhpur, with George hoping there was no strong wind to wreck his compass readings. After refuelling all was well to Allahabad with brilliant sunshine and first-rate visibility, although the thermometer had risen to 112° F. Approaching Calcutta there were great banks of cumulus clouds on the horizon and on landing they discovered the airfield had been flooded by the deluge. This was the monsoon season, George noting:

> What a name to conjure with and one that makes brave men stay at home and others wish they had. I had heard such a lot about this monsoon business before leaving England that I was more than interested to meet it face to face.

And he did!

The intention was to make Rangoon but, after take-off from Calcutta the Envoy entered the first storm. George needed all his strength to keep the aircraft on course, where he considered the rudder was influenced more by rain than airflow. Over the Bay of Bengal conditions improved with visibility rising to 500 feet. A meteorological report showed that rainfall along the Burmese coast was 15 inches in nine hours, something that George had never encountered before. The cocoa trees were bending well in the storm, with George beginning to grow weary whilst controlling the aircraft. Akyab was spotted and George was pleased that the runway was still above water. After landing he noted that both he and the cabin were saturated. Whilst refuelling George surveyed the paint-stripped wing's leading edges and engine cowlings – nature was in control. However, he decided to press on to Rangoon as the rain was easing. He learnt that Amelia Earhart had passed through three days before and had had to make three attempts to get away from Akyab. On approaching Rangoon there was another tropical thunderstorm in progress but the airfield was soon located:

> We skirted up and down until the storm moved off, then landed. A kind Shell representative took me for a drive to see the wonders of the city but, as it was dark, I fell asleep almost immediately.

Things were not looking good the following morning, but George decided to push on, only to find the weather was worse:

> Never have I seen such rain. It streamed down into the cabin although all the windows were shut, soaking everything. Then I noticed something quite new – the RPM indicators were filling up with water inside. All the fuses blew and I don't blame them one bit. For a time things looked a bit gloomy as we crossed the Gulf of Martaban. I think any monsooning aviator will tell you that this section can be absolute hell. Large ships are held up by the rain but the trusty Cheetah engines stuck at it. After a steady climb aided by Messrs Sperry I found Bangkok more or less clear.

The next morning was a well-needed rest prior to setting off for Hanoi. A large mountain range had to be crossed, which entailed further storms, but with the aid of the Sperry equipment they climbed into magnificent cloud scenery prior to crossing the coast of the China Sea. Then a final run northward to reach Hanoi. George was keen to press on to Hong Kong but was delayed by diplomatic paperwork. As the course took them over China, the routing was arranged by the Chinese government. For some reason he had to fly via two settlements in China before reaching Hong Kong. George's map did not cover this area and the Chinese Consul took two days to obtain the necessary information and maps, plus providing a local navigator:

> I took off on a northerly course through attractive mountain scenery which quickly clouded up. Some nifty aerobatics were necessary to get down the narrow valley which housed the first hamlet astride a river. A message was dropped and the Chinese ran for their lives, apparently deluded that it was a bomb. No shots were fired and we climbed away through the clouds to repeat the performance at the next hamlet. I was glad of our 1,000 mile range as this game of hunt the slipper amongst cloud covered mountain ranges, plus a funny map, can be expensive on fuel. I had a 500 mile run to do for Hong Kong with no hope of any landings.

All was well and Kai-Tak was reached mid-afternoon. Someone pleased to see them was Bill Dudman, the local Airspeed representative.

The arrival of the two Englishmen was reported in the *Hongkong Daily Press*, describing how George had battled with unfavourable weather, tropical sandstorms and monsoon rains. The Envoy was reported as having the most modern blind flying instruments, radio, homing device and oxygen for high-altitude flying. 'If only', commented George. Surveying the aircraft again, it was in no fit state to be delivered to its new owner, so it was into the hangar for a quick respray and check over, during which time another typhoon passed by. George had run out of his maps, as the Ordnance Survey had nothing available for central China. Luckily, he managed to borrow an old German survey map, some thirty-three years out of date. The Envoy departed on 7 July for the final 350-mile run northwards to Liu Chow, passing over desolate mountain ranges and encountering further storms. An Air Force pilot was carried to guide them, but he was more interested in the luggage he was carrying home from Hong Kong. George noted there was an enormous leather trunk, a large wireless set, a box filled with rifles, another with ammunition and lastly a barrel of gunpowder. George reasonably considered the aircraft was well over its overload weight, but it had no problem taking off. So, at last, the Envoy reached its destination:

> The Chinese were distinctly pleased with the speedy delivery of their aeroplane. We were received kindly and hospitably, and although we never fully mastered the chopstick technique, I have the pleasantest recollections of Kwangsi Province.

Having safely arrived at Liu Chow, George undertook a number of other flights. The Envoy was flown to Sao Yu for a demonstration to the family of the local military chief of staff. Taking off on the grass strip one wheel hit a sunken concrete block, resulting in a burst tyre, although George made a safe landing. Whilst the wheel and tyre were repaired George returned to Liu Chow by road. At the invitation of the local General he undertook a flight in the Kwangsi Type 3 single-seat biplane fighter. This prototype had been built by the Kwangsi Government Aircraft Factory and initial flights showed poor performance. George described it as a G.22 and considered it resembled a Blackburn Lincock. Powered by an Armstrong Siddeley Cheetah, as was the Envoy, the General felt that George was well placed to establish why the fighter failed to reach its design speed. However, in the short time available, George was unable to solve the problem. The Envoy caught up with him and he flew an acceptance flight for the Governor on 10 July. Early on 12 July George gave conversion training to two local air force pilots before flying the Envoy down to Wuchow as the first stage of his return to England. Here the landing ground was alongside the West River, which disappeared at times of high water! George left the Envoy in the hands of the local pilots; unconfirmed reports say it crashed less than a year later. George had a two-day boat ride from Wuchow down the West River to Hong Kong. For his safety, and that of other 'ransomable passengers', he spent most of the time in a locked cage with planks as a bed! He was glad to get away from Hong Kong.

The Envoy's delivery proved to be George's longest ever flight as sole pilot, a total of 9,300 miles. *Flight* magazine described it as the longest delivery flight, almost forgetting Percy's earlier flight. During this time George had carried out all aircraft and engine maintenance. Most of the navigation was by dead reckoning as he had no radio and out of date maps that only went as far as Hong Kong. On his return home, reports and photographs of his exploits were published in the *Illustrated London News* as well as *The Aeroplane*.

Preparing the second Chinese Envoy G-AEXE at Portsmouth in June 1937, prior to George's long delivery flight.

Refuelling Envoy G-AEXE at Jodhpur, Rajasthan, en route to Allahabad (now Prayagraj).

The reception party for the crew at Hong Kong, where the Envoy required attention before flying on to its Chinese destination.

With George's interest in clouds, he had to photograph this formation as the Envoy passed over the West River in southern China.

Whilst at Liu Chow in China, George undertook a test flight of this locally produced Kwangsi Type 3 fighter. Its performance proved unspectacular.

Chapter 5

Military Orders

Airspeed obtained a contract to build a radio-controlled, pilotless aircraft for the RAF and Royal Navy. Two prototypes of the AS30 Queen Wasp were ordered in May 1936 with K8887 making its maiden flight on 11 June 1937, piloted by George. His logbook notes this as 'Queen Wasp Target A/C markings V39', with serial K8887 added to the book later. As he was away in China, further testing was carried out by Percy, including the first flight of float-equipped K8888 from Lee-on-Solent in November. On his return, George flew K8887 on a number of tests, describing it as 'Target K8887', and on 19 October he flew 'Target K8888', now fitted with wheels. The Queen Wasp could be catapulted, either as a landplane or floatplane. Landplane trials were undertaken at Farnborough in April 1938 with K8888 wrecked during one catapult test. The acceleration force broke the pilot's seat backrest, resulting in the pilot being thrown backwards – unable to control the aircraft. George noted that it had 'been written-off having made a three-point landing on its engine and two wings'. In fact, it returned to Portsmouth for a major rebuild. George discovered a strange phenomenon whilst flying K8887 on stalling trials and demonstrated it to Hessell one day. Flying over Portsmouth Airfield at 2,000 feet George throttled back and pulled the stick back to adjust the angle of incidence. Speed dropped through 45 mph to nil, with height lost, but George still had full control. He told Hessell that by applying full aileron the Queen Wasp would gently rock as if undertaking normal flying. However, Hessell felt they were in a super stall condition, dropping vertically and perhaps even flying backwards. George finally opened up the throttle before they reached the ground, skimmed a hedge and landed back on the airfield.

With Envoy sales under their belt, Airspeed was approached by the Air Ministry to submit the design to meet the requirements of a new RAF trainer. On the face of it the existing airframe was suitable but in reality, much redesign work was needed for the resulting Oxford. An order was placed in October 1936 with the prototype L4534 flown by Percy on 19 June 1937 (five days after George had departed for China). On his return George first flew an Oxford on 8 August, undertaking various trials during the summer. On 29 September George flew it on its final acceptance test prior to being handed over to the RAE at Farnborough. By that time the first production Oxford was ready, so George took it on its maiden flight on 11 November. Two more followed by mid-December – all being delivered to the Central Flying School. Anticipating further orders, Airspeed realised they could not produce sufficient Oxfords at Portsmouth. So, in June 1938, the Air Ministry arranged for them to be built by de Havilland Aircraft at Hatfield, Percival

Aircraft at Luton and Standard Motors at Coventry. George found it 'rather ironic that the old enemy (de Havilland) had been detailed to make 200'.

George was reunited with his Swift when Capt. Luxmoore let him borrow it on 9 October 1937 for a flight to Leamington via Shuckburgh Park. George realised he needed a replacement 'field aeroplane' and spotted BA Swallow G-AEZM for sale. After overhaul, it was test flown by George on 7 May 1938, prior to flying to the Royal Aeronautical Society Garden Party at Heathrow the following day. The term 'Garden Party' did not do the event justice – it was more like a Farnborough Air Show of the 1950s. George took a two-week break at the beginning of June, which was spent on an intensive gliding course at the London Gliding Club, under the guidance of their Chief Instructor, H. E. Hervey. George flew to Dunstable Downs in his Swallow to begin the course with hops in a Primary, followed by winch launches. George soon progressed to a more advanced Grunau Baby, which he flew during the next five days. He undertook a duration flight of five hours three minutes on 10 June, which qualified him for his Silver C Gliding Certificate.

For his September holiday George undertook two further grand tours – the first to Denmark. On 3 September the Swallow departed Portsmouth for the usual customs clearance at Lympne and Le Zoute. He spent some time in Belgium before flying on to Amsterdam and Hamburg on 5 September, then stopping in Copenhagen. As with his 1935 trip, the local press reported on George's flight. It pointed out that George made it through the rain, whereas the airline service from Berlin was delayed because of the heavy thunderstorms. George departed Copenhagen on 8 September in the company of some Taylor Cubs from the Malmo Aeroklubb for a short hop to Kastrup. It was time to return on 12 September, but strong headwinds meant that George decided to stop off at Hamburg. Further headwinds the following day meant the Swallow took over four hours to reach Amsterdam, followed by a push on to Le Zoute. After a night stop it was off to Lympne and a return to Portsmouth, where a new tour commenced that evening, taking him to Tedsmore Hall. A few days were spent here, with day trips to Woodford, Combermere Abbey and Shawbury for a RAF visit on 19 September. In the afternoon it was on to Bagington, adjacent Whitley Abbey, Leamington and Castle Combe. The next day was South Cerney (where Oxfords were being delivered to No. 3 SFTS), flying in low cloud and rain, before finally returning to Portsmouth where an Oxford awaited a check flight. George must have been worn out! If he wanted to get away from things, he found it best to drive into the countryside and go for a long walk.

There were problems at Airspeed with disagreements between the 'old' and 'new' board members and in the spring of 1938, it appeared that Hessell was going to resign. However, he was persuaded to stay, and it was Nevil who departed in April on 'gardening leave'. He went on to develop his reputation as best-selling author Nevil Shute with Hessell appointed Managing Director. Having 'lost' his ally, George also considered moving on. He contacted colleague Arthur 'Clou' Clouston at RAE Farnborough in July concerning the possibility of becoming a civilian test pilot there. 'Clou' replied that Farnborough were not certain what they wanted at the time, so George decided to remain with Airspeed. He was pleased to learn in September that Nevil had finally obtained his pilot's licence.

Early 1938 saw George undertake the first flight of Oxfords as they came off the production line followed by production flight testing, prior to delivery to the RAF. After the excitements of South Africa and China this was mundane, but necessary, work. Amongst the multitude of military 'first flight tests' and 'check tests', there was the testing of Oxford G-AFFM in August. It was fitted with additional wireless equipment for trials by British Airways on behalf of the Director of Civil Aviation. Two Envoys then required testing. These had been ordered for the Air Officer Commanding RAF India in Delhi. George flew them during August, prior to their being flown out to Delhi. For a bit more excitement George visited RAF Bicester on 22 August. Here he was given a fifteen-minute flight in a Blenheim I by Sqd Ldr Christopher Paul of 90 Squadron. It was then a rather hairy flight on 30 September as George visited Hanworth, where he was given a twenty-five-minute flight in a Cierva C30 autogyro. In his logbook he noted 'First flight in Giro'. More rural trips in the Swallow followed with a visit to Winterborne Stickland on 15 October where George landed in a stubble field complete with hare. Then on to a meadow adjacent to Moyles Court House, giving friends joy flights the following day. It was off to Le Bourget on 3 December, via the usual customs clearance at Lympne. George spent two days at the Paris Air Show, which was held in the Grand Palais, Champs Elysees. Britain was represented by a Blenheim, Hurricane and Spitfire. George was later than anticipated returning home and found it turning dark whilst still over Sussex. So, he stopped off at Ford for the night, finally making Portsmouth the following afternoon.

Airspeed undertook a one-off job at the end of 1938. The Alvis Car Company had branched out in aero engines and developed the 450 hp 9ARS radial piston engine – later named the Leonides. After ground testing at Coventry it needed to be flight tested, so Airspeed were awarded the contract to install it in Bristol Bulldog K3183. The Bulldog was first flown by George on 19 January 1939 and further trials followed. On the afternoon of 16 February it was flown to Coventry by George to be demonstrated to the Alvis workforce, with Percy in the back seat. Both attended the Alvis staff dinner dance that evening, along with Hessell Tiltman, with George expressing his entire satisfaction with the new engine. Testing from Portsmouth continued during February and March, demonstrating that the new engine did not leak oil during flight, as was the case with the majority of engines in service at the time. At the end of one flight the propeller spinner fell off over Langstone Harbour. George circled the area and thought he spotted the spinner, so landed the Bulldog at Portsmouth, jumped into his Swallow and set off. He landed on a sandbank, only to find that what he thought was the spinner was an old oil drum. Meanwhile the airfield staff had reported an aircraft crashing into the harbour and called the rescue boat out. The crew were then astonished to see the Swallow rise from the sandbank and return home. One memorable flight was a demonstration to John Marlow from Alvis. George decided to climb through the prevailing cumulonimbus clouds, thinking they would prove no problem for the overpowered Bulldog. Passing 17,000 feet, George noticed ice building up on the struts, pitot head and the venturi tube powering the blind flying instruments. Unconcerned about the immense power of the clouds he was flying through, George flew on by the seat of his pants until he realised Marlow was shouting out in panic. On looking at him George was puzzled as he appeared to be suspended upside down in his safety harness. Only then did George realise the Bulldog was in an inverted dive! Control was regained as the Bulldog levelled out rather too close to Chichester Cathedral for comfort. George concluded that if he was to fly old crates by the seat of his pants, he needed to be sure that his seat was in contact with the old crate at all times. Test flying continued, but unfortunately for Alvis, war delayed development of their engine by ten years.

The Minister of State for Air, Sir Kingsley Wood, visited the Airspeed factory on the morning of 30 January 1939. He toured the Oxford production line, saw the King's Flight Envoy, the Queen Wasp and watched as George demonstrated an Oxford. The new year saw Oxford testing away from Portsmouth, these being the aircraft produced by de Havilland Aircraft, Percival Aircraft and Standard Motors. The first Oxford from Hatfield was ready at the beginning of 1939 and George was tasked with flying it, also catching up with news from Geoffrey de Havilland. Whilst there, George managed to fly as co-pilot to Geoffrey on the test of a Flamingo airliner, practise stalls on a Dragon Rapide prior to its delivery to Airwork, complete stalling tests on a Don and general flying on a Moth Minor. A Harvard I arrived at Portsmouth in the middle of May, with George flying it on handling tests in connection with the forthcoming AS45 trainer. On the afternoon of the 25 May, he delivered the Harvard back to Martlesham Heath, stopping off at Hatfield. Here George received a request from Geoffrey concerning Hatfield-built Oxfords. Local airspace restrictions meant that engine performance testing could not take place above 3,000 feet and that to fly higher meant taking the aircraft further away over Hereford and Worcester. Geoffrey considered this a waste of time and would George agree that limited testing would be satisfactory to pass Oxfords out? George advised what the de Havilland pilots should look out for on the engine instruments to indicate if they were operating correctly. He explained that his testing was carried out over the Channel, south of the Isle of Wight. The problem was that if he had to bail out there would be a long swim home. Also, the navy gunners at Fort Cumberland would sometimes fire at target drogues, only for their shells to carry on into the Oxford testing area. All part of the joys of being a test pilot!

George's Swallow was much in demand, taking him from one end of the country to the other. On the afternoon of 17 March 1939, he flew up to Gatwick where he attended 19 ERFTS's dinner and dance. Then, on the morning of 28 March, he made one of his regular visits to Tedsmore Hall, but bad weather forced him to land at Shawbury. The 7 April saw the start of a West Country trip, initially landing at Huish Hill, near Marlborough, to check out the local gliding site. It was then on to Barnstable and Weston-super-Mare, taking in views of the North Devon Coast en route. The following morning George flew across to Lundy Island, returning to Barnstable for a couple of nights' rest. The return trip to Portsmouth included stopping the night at Moyles Court. He returned to Moyles Court again on 25 April, giving joy rides to friends before returning to Portsmouth with his sister on board. George started a week's holiday, first flying to Tedsmore Hall on 26 May, then to Sutton Bank Gliding Camp, home of the Yorkshire Gliding Club. From here he made a short hop to visit Major J. E. D. Shaw of Slingsby Sailplanes, at Kirbymoorside. Whilst there he witnessed a gliding crash on 30 May and, being a test pilot, was called up to give expert evidence. An Avro Cadet had taken off towing a Slingsby Gull. George saw the Gull reaching a greater height than the Cadet, affecting the angle of the tow rope, which then pulled up the tail of the Cadet. The pilot was unable to correct the resulting dive in which both aircraft were destroyed on hitting the ground. Not the best memory of a holiday. Later George wrote a letter to the *Sailplane Magazine* concerning the accident and giving his thoughts on what lessons should be learned by future pilots. This was appreciated by Fred Slingsby, Slingsby Sailplanes' founding director. He thanked George in a letter, ending:

> We all enjoyed your company. Sorry your holiday was muddled up by crashery, but it was a godsend you were here to give such valuable assistance.

In May, George arranged with his contact at Flight Refuelling for the Swallow to be fitted with landing lights in the wings, as they would assist with any night flying. These proved useful in the summer when the Swallow was flown on Army Co-operation flights for 5th AA Unit. On 26 June, George flew it around the Guildford area until after midnight, on the following night around Winchester and on 4 July around Winchester and Selsey Bill, again until after midnight.

> I was delighted with the night experience and the fascination of riding amongst the clouds on moonlight nights while the searchlights wandered everywhere in the sky but in the right spot. Many times I went off course to fly into their beam just to encourage the exasperated operators below.

On 2 July 1939 George flew Oxford G-AFVS to Evere, Brussels, where it was displayed indoors at the city's Aero Exhibition before being taken over by the Belgium Air Force in August for trials. The Queen Wasp prototypes were further tested by George during May and June 1939. On 26 June he flew K8887 up to Farnborough so that he could collect K8888 and return it to Lee–on-Solent where it was refitted with floats. On 29 June he attended the MAEE Felixstowe where he received instruction from F/O Dennis on a Fairey Seal floatplane, followed up by his first solo flight in a floatplane. This was in preparation for his test flying the float-equipped Queen Wasp. Further tests were undertaken before he delivered it to Felixstowe on 12 July for sea trials.

Prior to entering RAF service, the Oxford had been subjected to spinning trials, something that was rare at the time for an aircraft of its size. Despite the trials, there were a number of fatal accidents involving trainee pilots who failed to recover from spins. Naturally the air force was not happy about these fatalities. As a result, Airspeed modified N6327 to have twin fins and rudders, so increasing the vertical area of the tail. It was flown by George on the evening of 14 July 1939, followed by trials of varying Centre of Gravity positions and stability trials. Spinning trials commenced at the beginning of September and all went well until the early afternoon of 16 September. Strangely, the day before, George had written to Geoffrey de Havilland saying, 'Spinning trials going along satisfactorily.' If only he had known! The aircraft was at full load with its C of G behind the aft limit. George put the Oxford into a spin at 16,000 feet and attempted recovery at 12,000 feet but failed with the aircraft continuing to spin out of control. It had fallen to 8,000 feet before George was able to activate the anti-spin parachute, which did not appear to work. George decided he should bail out, but on reaching the cabin door realised that the aircraft was recovering. He returned to his seat and pulled the anti-spin parachute lever again – still without any effect. George was now in a sweat and decided he would definitely bail out. He later recounted:

> We sorted that one out and found ourselves in cloud, with plenty on the clock, a great noise from the whirling 'paddles' and in a vertical position. I was now only partly engrossed in driving as I was trying to get out and walk. Then the parachute pulled clear, breaking a tail plane fitting en route. So I returned to the controls and we came out of cloud in one mighty swipe, just missing the top of a hill near Cullompton.

It was not realised at the time that he was the first pilot to save an aircraft by using its anti-spin parachute – even if inadvertently. George regarded this as his nearest squeak whilst Chief Test Pilot for Airspeed. Later in the month he was very relived to deliver N6327 to the boffins at RAE Farnborough where its spinning tests continued.

As well as corresponding with Thurston James at *The Aeroplane* magazine (Thurston was also Air Correspondent of *The Sunday Times*), George had also been introduced to Peter Masefield, who was appointed the magazine's Technical Editor in 1939. Peter asked him to write an item relating to his flying experiences, whereupon George replied, 'Only one thing is more dangerous than flying an Avro 504K against a strong headwind and that is writing something on practical flying in an Aeronautical Journal.' Typical George thinking. Nevertheless he did write the article.

George with the prototype Queen Wasp target aircraft K8887 at Portsmouth in June 1937.

The second prototype Queen Wasp K8888 was fitted with floats and is seen taking off from the Solent, off Lee-on-Solent.

The sorry state of Queen Wasp K8888 after its take-off incident at Farnborough. Airspeed pilots were not flying it at the time.

George oversaw the testing of many Envoys prior to delivery to foreign customers. F-AQAA was one of five for Air Pyrénées in 1937.

The prototype Oxford L4534 at the RAF Hendon Display in 1937, equipped with a mock-up gun turret.

The Oxford final assembly line at Portsmouth in the autumn of 1938 – the third for New Zealand is on the left.

High over Hampshire in the spring of 1938, George is in the left-hand seat of an early Oxford.

Courier K4047 was destined for experimental work at RAE Farnborough. George flew it between Portsmouth and Farnborough on a number of occasions.

The King's Flight ordered Envoy G-AEXX with George giving instruction to Wg Cdr Fielden, the Flight's Captain, during the spring of 1937.

George aboard Bristol Bulldog test bed K3183, fitted with a 450 hp Alvis Leonides engine and first flown by him in January 1939.

Seen at Portsmouth prior to a test flight, a well-wrapped-up George examines the new Leonides engine.

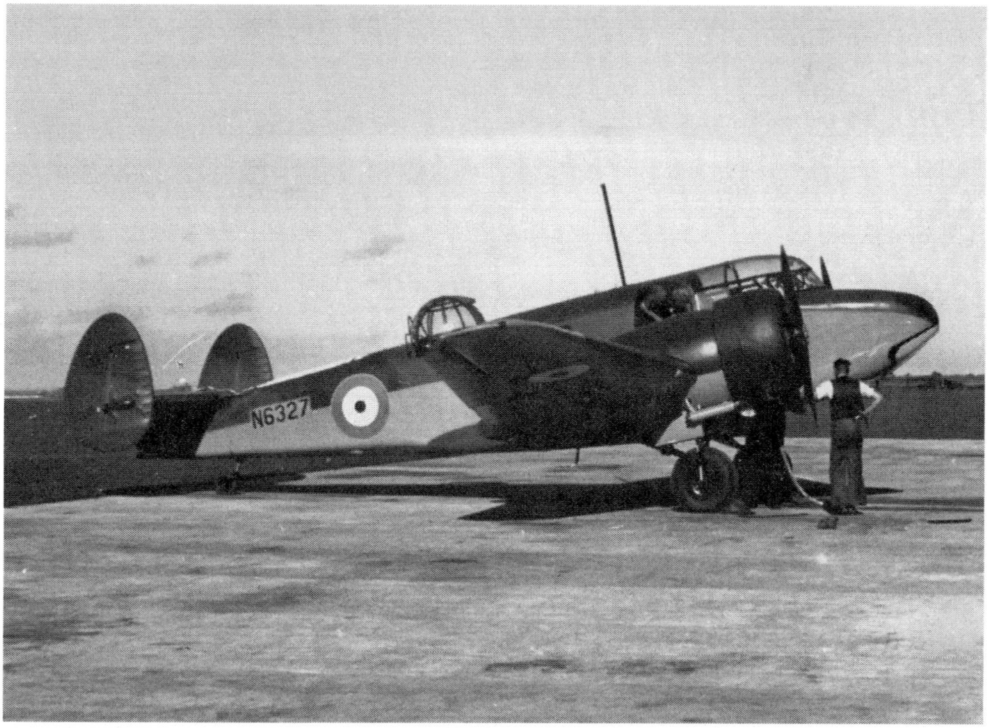

The experimental twin-finned Oxford, N6327, that gave George problems whilst test flying over Devon in July 1939.

George's father, mother and sister with his Swallow G-AEZM in a field adjacent to Moyles Court House, Ringwood.

A view from the cockpit as George overflies Moyles Court House, which was a frequent destination for him in the late 1930s.

The gliding crash at Kirbymoorside, witnessed by George in May 1939. The wrecked Gull is in the foreground with the Cadet in the far field.

Chapter 6

Early Days of the Second World War

Following the outbreak of war in September 1939 test flying from Portsmouth continued much as before. After a few months Percy Colman decided to rejoin the RAF, resulting in George being appointed Airspeed's Chief Test Pilot in the spring of 1940. His logbook continues with numerous entries of 'first flight test' and 'check test' of Oxfords. Around the same time Ron Clear, who had joined Airspeed in 1936 as an engine fitter, became a check production pilot on Oxfords. He had been the Oxford liaison engineer between Airspeed and the RAF, being involved in the initial deliveries. George visited Luton on 26 October to fly the first Oxford II produced by Percival Aircraft. Otherwise George's only break from Oxfords was test flying an Envoy on 24 October, following its rebuild, plus a flight in a new Vega Gull, whilst at Luton. To end 1939, George undertook continued testing of the Queen Wasp prototype at Lee-on-Solent, ending the year with over 1,500 hours in his logbook.

A batch of Oxfords had been produced for RNZAF and, as well as flight testing, George delivered a number to Hornchurch or Speke early in 1940 where they were packed for shipment. Iran also received three Oxfords and, as well as test flights, George gave flight instruction to Capt. Hafiz of the Iranian Air Force. George delivered the first two to Hanworth where they were packed for dispatch to Iran. A flight by Oxford to Hornchurch on 2 August included a stop off at Hatfield, where George undertook a twenty-minute general handling in 'DH Experimental 98' – the Mosquito. This is what George noted in his logbook, but it cannot have been the Mosquito. At the time the prototype was still being constructed at Salisbury Hall, not arriving at Hatfield until November prior to its maiden flight on 25 November. George's logbook entry has 'Mosquito' added later in pencil and then underlined in red. Shortly after the war George wrote to colleague Geoffrey Dorman saying that:

> On 2 August 1940 he flew the DH 98 and straight-way expressed his humble opinion to de Havilland father and son that this must be the best aeroplane in the world.

So, a puzzle remains as to what George actually flew.

Back in the summer of 1939 George had visited Flight Refuelling at Ford at the request of Sir Alan Cobham, who was looking for a stand-by pilot for experimental work and thought George would be willing to 'have a go'. During his 'spare time' he was given flight instruction by Sir Alan and test pilot Geoffrey Tyson on the AW23 bomber/transport in connection with proposed flight refuelling tests. On 15 February 1940, George refreshed his acquaintance with AW23 G-AFRX in preparation for the real trials, which he described as 'all quite good fun and something out of the ordinary'. George and Geoffrey flew the AW23 from Ford to Boscombe Down on the afternoon of 24 February, where it was involved in night-time refuelling trials. The plan was to commence trials on a moonlit night, then progress to darker ones, with George flying the AW23 and Geoffrey the accompanying Harrow tanker. Their first flight included some circuit training aided by mobile floodlights, as Boscombe's runway lights were not working. George recounted the refuelling as follows:

> At 11 pm all was set for the great adventure and off we went with Geoffrey intent on loading between 600 and 900 gallons of petrol. No wireless and no means of location. We had the benefit of a lamp rigged on my starboard wing to illuminate the top. We smelt *[sic]* about in an orderly manner in our ink black arena, and finally contacted each other. Everything went to plan; the harpoon contacting principle was ideally suited. I believe we established a bit of history by doing the first night air-refuelling over England and certainly the first under black-out conditions.

Further trials were carried out on the nights of 1 and 4 March to prove the principle was quite satisfactory. The success of these few flights encouraged Sir Alan and further trials were considered unnecessary. All this was accomplished without George having any heavy aircraft hours under his belt, let alone at night, no experience of formation flying or anything to do with flight refuelling, but he was still glad at being able to 'have a go'.

Airspeed was on the lookout for additional test pilots. In January 1940 George wrote to Eric Alliott Verdon-Roe (son of Avro's founder) offering him a job as George knew that his RAF commission ended in March. Although he was keen to join Airspeed, his promotion to Squadron Leader meant that he decided to remain in the RAF. Both Brian Field and Robert Milne joined as test pilots early in 1940, being mainly involved in Oxford test flying. In June, George moved lodgings to the Old Mill Cottage at Langstone. He recalls bombs dropping all around the area in September, but they missed the Old Mill, luckily. Changes to Airspeed's structure also occurred in June when de Havilland Aircraft bought out Swan Hunters shareholding. As a result, a number of de Havilland directors joined the Airspeed Board, with only Hessell Tiltman remaining from the original days. With these changes, the Airspeed design team were moved to Hatfield in 1940, as Portsmouth was considered in the front line for enemy attacks. In fact, it was the Hatfield design office building that was destroyed by the Luftwaffe!

Spitfire K9386 arrived from Eastleigh on 16 March 1940 and George was able to have an hour's flight in it. The fighter was on loan to Airspeed for trials and George managed a further thirty-five minutes a couple of days later. This was a whole new experience – flying a modern high-speed fighter compared with a sedate Oxford. He flew it again on 11 May before being given the chance to deliver it to Llandow, South Wales, later in the afternoon. Feeling like a schoolboy who had just had an exceptional treat he sent a postcard to his sister saying how he had flown from Portsmouth to Llandow in twenty-seven minutes (it seems strange that such Spitfire information escaped the wartime censor). He then went walking with a family friend around the Ogmore Castle area before returning by train. The RAF's first production Queen Wasp P5441 was flown by George on 29 March and engine installation tests were carried out during April. It was delivered to Hawkinge on 17 April, with George giving instruction to RAF pilots of the Pilotless Aircraft Unit the following day. With production just getting underway, Airspeed were informed by the Air Ministry that the aircraft were no longer required and the order for 323 was cancelled. Despite this, flight testing continued at Portsmouth and Farnborough. Strangely, a 1941 Airspeed advert showed an image of a camouflaged Royal Navy Queen Wasp being catapulted off a warship.

Airspeed then produced another one-off type. The AS39 had been designed to a demanding specification for a slow-flying aircraft able to undertake night-time observation, operating from an aircraft carrier. The resulting Night Shadower was a strange-looking high-wing design powered by four Pobjoy Niagara engines. Prototype N1323 was completed by August 1940, with George undertaking taxiing trials at Portsmouth on 10 August. It was back to the hangars for modifications before George took it up for its maiden flight on 17 October. The aircraft then had woollen tufts applied, for stalling tests, during October and November. Modifications were made to the engine mounts and their cowls to try and improve its flying ability. Low-speed tests confirmed the instability of the aircraft and George was not complimentary about the Night Shadower. He initially referred to it by this name, although it was later more commonly referred to as the Fleet Shadower – the same name as the General Aircraft competing design. George described its rate of climb as negligible, elevator control having much to be desired, excessive drag due to the basic design, a nose down attitude at lower speed which, if uncontrolled, developed into a stall at around 35 mph. In a letter to a fellow test pilot at Hatfield he described the Fleet Shadower:

> [It is] the purest form of a flying basket yet devised with a gliding angle rather similar to that of a tomb stone dropped out of a balloon, that is if you can find an aeronaut who flies a balloon complete with his own tomb stone.

The project was cancelled by the Air Ministry, although George was still flying N1323 in May 1941. A second prototype was never completed, and the General Aircraft design also disappeared into oblivion. All the staff at Airspeed were distressed to receive the news that Percy Colman had been killed when his Blenheim had been shot down off Worthing on the night of 3/4 January 1941. At the time he was Acting Squadron Leader with 23 Squadron – George had lost a good friend.

Towards the end of September 1940, George received an urgent phone call to say his parent's home, Old Stacks, had been hit during an attack by a lone Junkers Ju88. It made four passes around the area before dropping its bombs, resulting in the house being completely destroyed in a spectacular explosion. Luckily George's parents were in the garden at the time, his mother receiving some cuts, but George and the family lost all their belongings. This was the only private property in Ringwood destroyed during the war and a 'story' emerged as to why. Prior to the war, William Joyce of the National Socialist League lived in Ringwood and knew the Errington family. Joyce left England for Germany in August 1939 and, as 'Lord Haw-Haw', broadcast propaganda messages to England on behalf of the Germans. The 'story' said that Luftwaffe pilots were instructed by 'Lord Haw-Haw' to bomb Old Stacks as he had fallen out with the elderly Mr Errington and it was also the home of an important British test pilot – a good wartime story but proved most unlikely afterwards. The family moved to Cookham near Maidenhead to stay with relatives.

Having delivered an Oxford to Stafford on the morning of 15 October 1940, George made his way over to Hatfield. Here he collected Mew Gull E.1 and flew it back to Portsmouth, undertaking handling tests en route. On 25 October he flew the Mew Gull up to Cambridge where he flight-tested Oxford L9660, which had been rebuilt by Marshall. From November George borrowed Miles Falcon G-ADLI as a run-about. It undertook flights to the likes of Farnborough, Hatfield, Cambridge, Cranwell and St Athan. Whilst returning from Colerne, on 16 March 1941, he ran into thick fog near the coast and ended up making a forced landing at Thorney Island, returning home the next day. Despite being wartime, George retained his Swallow and was allowed to fly it with its civilian registration. No doubt he persuaded the Ministry that it was essential for Airspeed's war effort, although it had to be camouflaged.

Airspeed had been instructed by the Air Ministry to design a high-performance RAF trainer in case there were delays with Harvards being received from America. The result was the AS45 Cambridge, with prototypes T2449/53 ordered in July 1939. The first was completed by February 1941 with George undertaking taxiing trials on 7 February. He took it up for its thirty-minute maiden flight on 19 February. Whilst on climbing tests on 18 March it suffered an engine failure, resulting in a forced landing at Worthy Down. He ferried it back three days later. George took the second prototype up for its maiden flight on 19 August and demonstrated it to Air Ministry VIPs two days later. George found that the Cambridge would not reach its designed diving speed of 330 mph, due to excessive drag. On one flight in T2453 during November, he pushed it to its limit of 270 mph before pulling out of the dive, whereupon much of the upper surface of the starboard wing came away:

> It happened that the outer section stayed on, which was considerate of it. The inboard top area vanished in a flash leaving an educational view like one of those revealing drawings one sees in the technical press. Controls and intact ribs were rudely exposed to the heavens and roaring gale. This was in no way a catastrophe. I felt some drag, some loss of lift and that was all.

George managed to safely land the Cambridge, although at a higher speed than normal. T2449 was tested by visiting A&AEE pilots during February and March 1942, but they found its handling unsatisfactory. George recorded his logbook as taking it up for aerobatics on 13 March, last noting it on 3 April 1943 undertaking aileron testing. It ended its days at Farnborough on non-flying trials.

In order to boost Oxford production, in 1940 Airspeed undertook the running of a new factory at Christchurch, which was officially opened in March 1941. George flew across from Portsmouth to undertake the flight of their first aircraft, X6520. The sole Oxford III P1864 was fitted with different Cheetah XV engines in the summer of 1940, although not test flown at Portsmouth by George until 7 April 1941. On 17 April he flew it on a general performance test to Hatfield and whilst there managed twenty-five minutes in the Mosquito prototype, W4050. Another one-off was Oxford AS504, fitted with Gipsy Queen engines. George carried out initial taxiing trials on 1 January 1942, whilst the first flight was undertaken by Ron Clear. Airspeed then developed the Oxford V with Pratt & Whitney engines for use in Canada. Prototype AS592 was converted from an Oxford I and was tested by George during May 1942. Many existing Oxfords were re-engined into this version with Ron sent to Canada to oversee deliveries to the training schools. By now there was less Oxford testing being undertaken by George as he was needed for other things. Further changes at Airspeed in 1942 saw Sir Alan Cobham step down as Director, shortly followed by Hessell Tiltman.

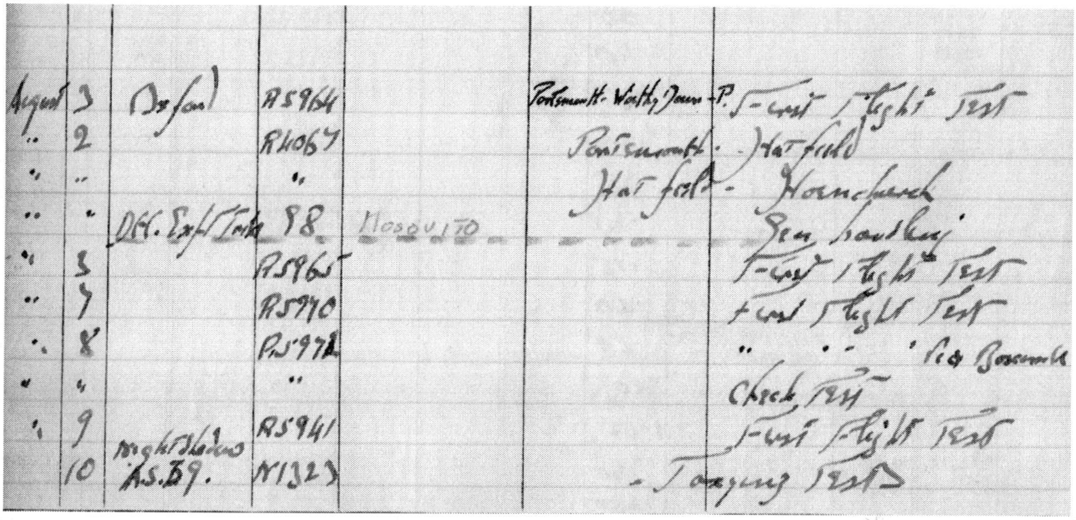

August	3	Oxford	AS964	Portsmouth-Worthy Down-P.	First flight test
..	2		R4067		Portsmouth - Hatfield
..	..		..		Hatfield - Hornchurch
..	..	DH. Expt Type	98	Mosquito	Gen handling
..	5		AS965		First flight test
..	7		AS970		First flight test
..	8		AS972		.. .. to Boscombe
..	..		..		Check test
..	9		AS941		First flight test
	10	Night Shadow AS.39.	N1323		Towing test

The logbook entry that shows George as having flown the DH Experimental 98 at Hatfield on 2 August 1940. He added Mosquito in pencil at a later date.

The AW23 K3585 flown by George on night-time flight refuelling trials at Boscombe Down in February 1940, where it successfully received fuel from a Harrow.

George seated in the cockpit atop the weird and ungainly AS39 Fleet Shadower N1323, at Portsmouth in August 1940.

A side view does not make the Fleet Shadower any less unsightly. George described its handling qualities as 'flying a tombstone'.

First flown by George in February 1941, the AS45 Cambridge trainer (named to compliment the Oxford) did not enter production. This is prototype T2449.

George, in white overalls, at Portsmouth for the handover of the 1,000th Oxford produced by Airspeed.

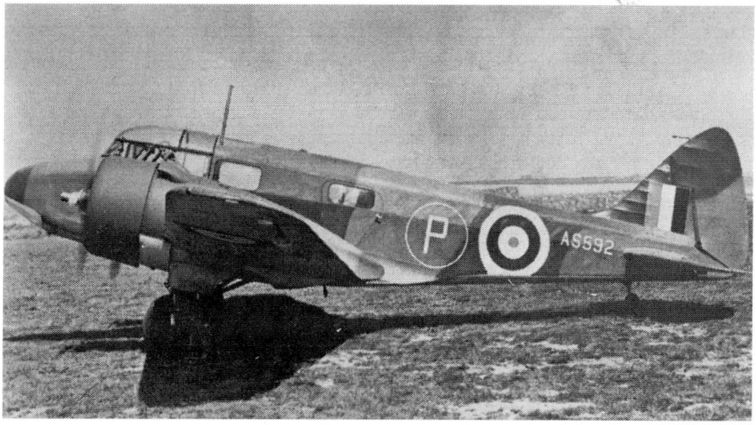

The prototype Oxford V AS592 was fitted with Pratt & Whitney engines for use with training schools in Canada.

The complete destruction of the Errington home, Old Stacks, at the hands of a Luftwaffe Ju88, in September 1940.

Chapter 7

Testing the Horsa

In January 1941 Airspeed designed the Horsa to the Ministry of Aircraft Production (MAP) requirement for a twenty-five-seat wooden troop-carrying glider. Airspeed seem to have been chosen as they had recently submitted a design for the AS48 wooden fighter, the MAP feeling that Airspeed would be better employed with this new requirement. Their design office was at London Colney and, following an order in February 1941 for four prototypes, a hangar was built there for construction of the first two. George was approached about flying the prototype as he was the only Airspeed test pilot with gliding experience, holding a Silver C Certificate. But, as he pointed out, this covered sailplanes not troop-carrying gliders. Another question was what aircraft would act as tug for the new glider? The Airspeed directors told George that he was to visit RAE Farnborough to obtain their advice. So, on 27 June, George met up with Sqd Ldr Hugh Wilson, Chief Test Pilot of the Aero Flight, to receive instruction on a Whitley bomber in use as a tug and on the Hotspur training glider.

The prototype Horsa DG597 was completed in August and taken to Fairey's Great West Aerodrome (which George described as Heathrow) for ground testing. On 27 August 1941, George flew up from Portsmouth in his Swallow to see the completed aircraft. A Whitley had also arrived as its tug and George spent some time seated in it towing the Horsa around the grass airfield. This involved Flt Lt W. R. H. 'Nick' Carter who had been loaned by RAE Farnborough to be the main Whitley pilot. Initially the combination would build up speed and then come to a halt. Later the Whitley took off, but the Horsa, with George in charge, cast off the towline and halted before the airfield boundary. At the time the RAF was establishing a glider training school and George flew to Haddenham on 11 September, where No. 1 Glider Training Squadron was equipped with Hawker Hector biplanes as tugs, and Hotspurs for training. George undertook flights in both types. This was prior to a more important event on the afternoon of the 12 September when George flew his Swallow back to Heathrow, where the Horsa awaited him. He was unhappy as the necessary paperwork had not been completed but, undeterred, he boarded the Horsa with Nick ready in the Whitley. However, the airfield's resident AID inspector said the flight would have to be cancelled due to the lack of correct paperwork. Despite this, the inspector was in his office and the pilots were in their aircraft, so, undeterred, both pilots decided to go for it. George undertook the Horsa's twenty-minute maiden flight with Sqd Ldr Wilson as his co-pilot. Those on the ground were concerned at the amount of runway needed before the combination became airborne. However, a safe flight and landing was made, with George undertaking further flights later in September and early October. The majority of the time would be undertaken whilst still under tow, only releasing the tow rope just prior to the end of each flight. Testing meant there was the need to get as much flight time in as possible. On one evening Nick estimated that there was enough fuel in the Whitley for the final flight of the day. After a short while heading towards London, and at 3,000 feet, the fuel ran out. Aware of the problem, George cast off the tow, commenting to Nick 'see you in Hyde Park'. Luckily both pilots made it safely back onto the grass at Heathrow.

With his experience building up, George was asked to take the Horsa to Baginton, which was Armstrong Whitworth's base. They wanted to undertake their tests on a Whitley in its role as a glider tug. On 25 November 1941, George piloted the Horsa under tow from the Whitley, piloted by Nick, to Baginton and for the next couple of days undertook unstuck trials at varying weights. To increase the payload George supervised the loading of concrete blocks or sandbags prior to each new test. Like Heathrow, Baginton only had a grass runway, so for a time the testing was moved to nearby RAF Honiley, which had a paved runway. On one occasion the Whitley/Horsa combination unintentionally entered cloud and George found he could see nothing. Initially he followed the vortex of the Whitley's engines, but this soon disappeared, leading to panic setting in. Not being able to see the Whitley, although still attached, George was hanging onto the control column like grim death, fearing that the Horsa would stall and crash. He later admitted this was another of 'the worst experiences of my career'. Eventually Nick lost height, George followed and soon both were out of the cloud and danger. Testing finished on 13 December, after which George returned the Horsa to Heathrow for modifications, prior to taking a Christmas break.

The second prototype Horsa, DG600, arrived at Heathrow at the end of January 1942, undertaking its first flight on 28 January, again with George at the controls. On 31 January he piloted it up to Baginton and then on 6 February, to RAF Snaith in Yorkshire. Here he demonstrated the glider to gathered Airborne Forces Experimental Establishment (AFEE) 'Brass', followed by familiarisation flights for AFEE pilots. Meanwhile, the third Horsa, DG604, had arrived at Christchurch, from where George undertook its first flight on 15 February, towing it over to nearby Hurn on 22 February. Testing confirmed that the Whitley struggled with the Horsa at higher weights, and so Halifaxes and Stirlings were tried as tugs. George undertook a familiarisation flight in a Halifax at Baginton on 28 February, and the following day it was used for the first time as a tug. Then, a Stirling was flown by George on 2 April, prior to its first use as a tug. Among the tests undertaken by George at Heathrow was to try varying lengths of rope between the tug and glider. Whilst trying a very long rope it sagged on take-off and dragged along the telegraph wires on the adjacent Great West Road. George felt this was like a violin bow in action producing a loud middle-C note that he felt sure could be heard as far away as Windsor Castle.

In 1942 it was decided that Netheravon on Salisbury Plain would be the new centre for airborne forces activity. George flew a Whitley up from Christchurch on 29 March in order to get approval to use the airfield. He then tested Horsa DG604 at Christchurch on 24 March with the intention of delivering it to Netheravon. But, on its final check flight, the undercarriage failed to jettison and then the Whitley tug suffered an engine failure. The flight ended with a forced landing back at Christchurch. All was in order the following day, with the Whitley towing the Horsa to Netheravon. George demonstrated the glider to a gathering of General Staff on 27 March and then to Churchill on 15 April. He flew the fourth Horsa, DG609, at Christchurch on 12 April, delivering it to AFEE Ringway on 30 April followed by DG604 on 1 May. During trials with a Whitley, a 'low tow' or 'high tow' position was developed for towing the Horsa, neither seeming to have any great benefit or disadvantage. However, with a Halifax or Stirling the Horsa pilot found to his disadvantage that he was constantly thrown between the low and high position, with the slipstream of the tug proving a constant battle. The problem was never successfully solved.

Despite having undertaken limited trials, the Horsa was ordered into full production by the MAP. As it was constructed from wood, the MAP arranged for production to be undertaken by non-aviation companies. George flew the first aircraft from the Harris Lebus furniture factory on 1 June, followed by the first from the Austin Motors factory, with the first Horsa built at Christchurch ready at the end of July. As production got underway, Horsas from Harris Lebus and Austin Motors were delivered by road to either No. 6 MU Brize Norton, No. 9 MU at Cosford or No. 51 MU at Lichfield to await their first flight. However, various Horsas from all three production lines found their way to Christchurch for testing by George and his colleagues. George regarded testing a penance after Oxford test flying. For every Horsa production test flight – the maximum duration of which normally did not exceed ten minutes – the Whitley tug and tow rope had to be found and then followed a combined take-off and climb to height. Every landing was a 'forced' landing, the tow rope had to be removed from the tug and the Horsa towed back to the hangar by tractor. Then the performance started all over again. As George became more adept, he found that time could be saved by releasing from the tug at 2,000 feet, diving to a maximum speed of 230 mph and swiftly landing from the pull out.

During Horsa testing there were a number of close shaves. Whilst undertaking a maximum load test with DG604, at Netheravon on 10 April 1942, George felt a jerk followed by a loud bang after dropping the undercarriage. His observer went back to the cabin but reported that he could see nothing untoward, so George proceeded with the planned diving trials. Unbeknown to those on board, the main undercarriage had bounced up and hit the rear fuselage under the tailplane, smashing a large hole in the structure. Quite how the tail stayed on during the maximum speed diving tests is something that George always considered as pure luck. He recalled the Horsa was snaking a lot due to there only being a limited amount of structure holding on the rear end. Whilst returning from Weston-on-the-Green to Netheravon on 14 June, the port undercarriage leg of the Horsa fell away as planned but the other wouldn't jettison. The flight test observers had 'great fun' throwing out 3 tons of concrete blocks to lighten the glider. This enabled George to bring off a one-wheel landing with barely a scratch to the fuselage. On another flight from Netheravon the ailerons became frozen and George had difficulty in controlling the Horsa. Using all his strength to control the glider's rolling flight by rudder alone, he ended up breaking the back off the pilot's seat. In the end he let go of the controls to enable fate to take its course. Luckily the Horsa made it back to Netheravon, bouncing over two haystacks in the process, finally coming to a safe halt. Ron Clear was flying the Halifax on a trial with George in the Horsa and communication was by a wireless cable attached to the tow rope. Successfully climbing through 16,000 feet, they had reached 20,000 feet over the Windsor area when Ron realised he was no longer in contact with George. The wireless cable had broken, and Ron observed the Horsa oscillating wildly and failing to keep station. George waved his white handkerchief out of the window by way of a SOS – it was later established that he had suffered oxygen starvation. Luckily George came around, cast off the tow and landed at Netheravon – some way from the intended Heathrow. Oxygen was installed for the next flight!

On a later date George was flying from Brize Norton down to Christchurch in a Whitley. There were some impressive cloud formations around, and he decided to try some blind flying practice in the clouds. Unfortunately, he failed to appreciate the strength of the wind within the clouds and ended up in the middle of Southampton's balloon barrage defence. He picked his way between the balloons, made it to the coast and headed east for safety. As he became more used to landing at Netheravon, George developed his own parking technique, which became regarded by others as his star turn. The Horsas were usually parked by a gully on the edge of the airfield known as Dead Man's Gulch by the Airspeed working party. George would land his Horsa up the side of the Gulch, let it roll back into a gap in the row and stop in line with the other Horsas. One of the Netheravon-based army pilots remarked:

> It was fun to fly with George in Horsas, not just to watch his impeccable handling, but to hear his absurdly comic patter, synchronised to the most bizarre manoeuvres.

Due to the Whitley's limitation as a tug, Airspeed was supplied with one of the prototype Halifax bombers at the end of 1941. It was overhauled at Portsmouth but was found to be worn out. After an engine failure and subsequent forced landing in January 1942, Airspeed demanded to be supplied with a brand-new Halifax as their tug – it soon arrived. With increased production of Oxfords and Horsas, George had a team of production test pilots to assist him – 'Nick' Carter, Ron Clear, Brian Field, Douglas Jones and Bob Milne. As required, they would fly over from Portsmouth to undertake Horsa and Oxford production test flights from Christchurch. Problems arose at Christchurch due to the limitations of the 2,400-feet grass runway, not aided by trees at its eastern end, and bungalows at the western end. The pilots refused to fly the Horsas out until the trees had been removed. They soon were! Early service trials were undertaken at Cranfield where one of the pilots came across what he regarded as a rogue Horsa. At certain speeds it adopted an erratic kind of roll and the pilot undertook his own diagnosis. By his calculations, the basic design had a lack of torsional stability, which could result in problems with all future Horsas. Airspeed were disturbed at this news and sent George up to Cranfield to undertake his own testing. Walking towards the aircraft George's experience solved the problem without the need for a test flight. He could see that, with the rudder centralised, the servo tab was fully displaced as a result of its connecting rod having broken. Panic over!

Sir Alan Cobham contacted George in August 1942 asking for his help on another Flight Refuelling project. The company had moved its offices from a blitzed Ford to Malvern with flying undertaken from Staverton. The new project was for a fighter to be towed by a larger aircraft in order to deliver the fighter over long distances. At the time there was a severe shortage of fighters in Malta and they lacked range to be flown from the nearest Allied bases. Sir Alan's plan was for a bomber and fighter to take off together, joined by a slack tow rope. Once at cruising height the tow rope would be fully deployed, and the fighter's engine switched off. The combination would then fly for two or three hours before the fighter restarted its engine, cast off the tow and flew to its destination. Initial trials were undertaken from Staverton with a Wellington and Hurricane, with Flight Refuelling pilot's perfecting the system. The RAF wanted demonstrations undertaken by other pilots, so Sir Alan called upon Jeffrey Quill from Supermarine, who knew a bit about fighters. Unfortunately, the tow rope snapped under the strain. Next it was the turn of Wing Cdr Hugh Wilson from RAE Farnborough, but his attempt ended in an early cast off when both aircraft were about to dive into the ground. Sir Alan then brought in George on 10 September, who managed to perform the task without any bother. After flying the Hurricane up to Defford, he spent forty-five minutes under tow from the Wellington. As Sir Alan pointed out, George did have a few hours' gliding experience in his logbook! However, the plan did not proceed as the RAF considered the task would be beyond the capability of the majority of its fighter pilots, although George considered they should have no particular difficulty. Further trials were undertaken using a Spitfire early in 1943. Although George did not get to fly the Spitfire, he continued to send his thoughts and observations on the testing to Sir Alan.

Prototype Horsa DG597, which was first flown by George on 12 September 1941 despite the paperwork not being complete. The location is what is now Heathrow Airport.

In the early days of Horsa testing it was normal for a Whitley to act as tug. Later, the greater power of a Halifax or Stirling was needed.

Rear fuselage damage to Horsa prototype DG604 at Netheravon, which caused worry to those on the ground who witnessed the incident in April 1942.

Dead Man's Gulch at Netheravon in 1942. Seen parked are three early Horsas with a Whitley and Halifax tug.

The Horsa Mk II had an opening nose which aided the loading of larger pieces of equipment such as this jeep.

View from the rear turret of a Halifax as a Horsa is towed aloft from Christchurch. The crosses on the wing indicate it is probably a test flight.

Chapter 8

Mosquitoes and Spitfires

By the end of 1942 Horsa development flying had been completed and, at Christchurch, it was now down to testing the gliders as they came off the production line. This was not going to tax George's skills and he wasn't happy with the standard of work given to him by Airspeed. Back on 11 September 1942 he had flown Mosquito IV DZ311 with Geoffrey de Havilland whilst on a visit to Hatfield and was then allowed thirty-five minutes' solo flying. Geoffrey was de Havilland's Chief Test Pilot, with plenty of work on his hands. During his time at Hatfield, George became a great admirer and friend of Geoffrey. Some of the Hatfield pilots had been sent to Toronto to test fly the Mosquitoes being built by de Havilland Canada. So, after pulling a few strings, George was loaned to de Havilland, reporting to Hatfield after Christmas 1942. He was tasked with testing Mosquito bombers and fighters as they rolled off the production line, so assisting the de Havilland family. George's first test flight on 30 December was a night fighter version, followed by a bomber the next day. Sometimes he would fly the Mosquito to Portsmouth as part of its shake-down flight. He then became involved in testing the high altitude NFXV version, which was fitted with Merlin 77 engines equipped with Stromberg carburettors. He was daily climbing to over 40,000 feet, 'which has always been a bit of a draw as far as I was concerned'. At that height he found there was little response from the control column with the Mosquito unable to climb further.

Richard Whittingham was a Mosquito inspector at Hatfield and recalls one of these test flights with George:

> On 16 February I was fortunate enough to go up in DZ417. When we reached 42,000 foot George reached across and switched off the pitot tube heater and immediately the Air Sped Indicator dropped to zero. He pointed at it and, as we were wearing oxygen masks and couldn't speak to each other, looked at me for an explanation. I switched the heater on again and, of course, the ASI went back to normal. George stuck his thumb up, but a few moments later did the same thing again. In the end I held my hand over the switch so he couldn't touch it. He then motioned that I should take over flying, whereupon he leaned back in the brilliant sunshine and shut his eyes. I had never flown anything before, let alone a Mosquito. I made a few tentative movements with the control column to find there was no response whatsoever. The Mosquito was wallowing about and unable to gain any more height. Fortunately the pilot 'woke up' and took over and we started to descend.

Mosquito testing only threw up one major problem for George, prior to his final test on 28 February 1943. The hiccup occurred whilst undertaking a slow roll on a production aircraft when its ailerons became jammed. George recounts the situation:

> I have always contended that the SBAC owe me a lot for presenting to the Hertfordshire public what could have been taken for a preview of aerobatics which were to be expected at the first SBAC show after the war. No one was more amazed than myself. It was only the Mosquito's adequate power reserve that kept the whole business respectable. Nevertheless it ended up in a series of gradually sloppier barrel rolls, decidedly on the decline, with Negative G imposed. A bolt had risen up out of the bowels of the Mosquito on the first roll and had become jammed in a chain over its sprocket. Things began to look decidedly serious when with the force born of despair I wrenched the wheel back to straight and thanked the Lord that I started the 'evolution' at a respectable height so enabling me to return safely to Hatfield.

Other new types for George included a Hawker Henley, which was at Hatfield for airscrew tests, and the Hawker Tornado prototype, which had been fitted with DH contra-rotating propellers.

There followed a period of sporadic flying at Portsmouth, with a few Horsa and Oxfords flown at the beginning of April 1943. Hearing that he still had little to do, Jeffrey Quill of Supermarines approached Airspeed to see if they would release George to assist in Spitfire testing. The directors agreed and so George reported to Supermarine at Worthy Down on 13 April. Development work was undertaken here on Spitfires and Seafires, away from the hassle of the main production lines. George's first test was an hour in Seafire IIc NM977 and, as well as acquainting himself with its handling, he undertook stability trials. Most Spitfire and Seafire testing was on aircraft with non-standard or new mark Merlin and Griffon engines. So much of George's work involved establishing how fast the aircraft took to climb to a certain height, and then trying to improve on the time. Special attention was paid to high-altitude pressurised Mk XIVs and XXIs, for example the Spitfire XXI prototype was flown to 50,000 feet. On 16 April he used a trials Spitfire IX to fly to Christchurch, where he undertook a flight test on Seafire IIc NM921. Airspeed was fitting a number of Seafires with new Merlin 32s and this was their first. A flight on the following day was brief as failure of the Merlin resulted in a forced landing:

> I was roaring along at full throttle near the Needles at some 2,000 foot and heading away from land when the engine seized up – an oil pipe having come off. I yanked the Seafire round and headed towards the coast, pulling it upwards with the remaining forward energy. With luck I could make land if everything kept up but I could not make Christchurch. I suddenly remembered the airfield just built at Holmsley South – I might reach there, but it was going to be a near go. By blowing the wheels down on the emergency system at the very last instant, and leaving the flaps up, I was just able to make the end of the brand new runway going downwind. It was some time before flying control realised that there was a silent visitor standing on their runway. I think I was almost the first aircraft to use the runway.

George frequently visited High Post where he undertook the first flight of a number of Spitfire XIIs. He got to fly Sea Otter amphibian prototype JN738 on 18 May and, after an hour of testing at Chattis Hill, flew it back to Worthy Down. Then on 25 May he undertook full-load trials with it, including a water landing on the Solent. Another Supermarine prototype was the Type 322 'Dumbo' R1810. An experimental aircraft, George described it in his logbook as the S24/37 – its Air Ministry Specification number. On 10 June he undertook flights with the variable incidence wing set at different angles, followed by stalling tests. In June, George reported that he found instability in the yaw which required adjustment to the rudder trim. With his engineering background and mathematical mind, George proved of great use to Supermarines. His main tasks had been to investigate the problem of Spitfire wing failures whilst on Mediterranean operations and engine fuel problems on high-flying PRU Spitfires. He solved both problems for Supermarine:

> The only untoward contingency concerned pressurised Spitfire VII EN494 which had a cockpit that was bolted from the outside and could not be undone by the pilot. Somewhere over Carmarthen on 2 June the engine stopped and I turned back towards Bath, where I selected Charmy Down to land at after my long glide. I force landed on the main runway and up came an excited and rather indignant 'attendant' in a jeep. He had never seen this type of Spitfire and I could not make him understand that I was unable to get out until he unbolted me. The canopy was such a good fit that nothing much could be heard through it. So I made signs for him to get cracking with a spanner. More and more aeroplanes joined the circuit, so they pushed me on to the grass and I went over it all again until they got the idea'.

George and the Spitfire later made it back to Worthy Down. In view of his useful work Jeffrey wanted George to stay on for a further three months, but this was not possible. Jeffrey commented, 'His experience and help, as well as conversation, was highly stimulating.' Another plus was the detailed reports George produced for each test, with a number of graphs showing engine performance at varying heights. George's final test for Supermarine was on 17 July when he took Spitfire XI EN654 to 41,000 feet. He had had an interesting few months carrying out development work on the fastest bomber in the world, followed by the fastest fighter – 'the happiest years of my test work'.

Returning to Portsmouth by the middle of July 1943, George undertook further Oxford flight testing, plus visits to Christchurch for Horsa flights. Having been unused for some time, George's Swallow made a few flights during the summer, but for business, not pleasure. He flew it over to Christchurch on 29 July where he test flew an Oxford and Horsa. Then on 30 August he flew up to Hatfield again where he spent a further five days flight testing Mosquito fighter-bombers. On 9 September Horsa HS104 was being towed back from Netheravon with George in the Halifax. Near Winchester, the Horsa, piloted by Bob Milne, was released in error and landed in a field at Morestead. George returned to Netheravon, switched to a Courier and flew back to Morestead to assess the problem. Following a phone call from a local farmer the police had swiftly arrived and, despite protests, arrested Bob and his co-pilot. The Horsa was then fenced off by the Army and Bob was unable to return to it. In the end the matter was resolved,

George was asked to rescue the Horsa and the following day he landed his Swallow in the field to check it over. He reported back to Portsmouth, who asked him to also check an adjacent field. Obviously, this proved satisfactory as later in the day he landed the Whitley tug, hitched up the Horsa and towed it back to Portsmouth. The new Halifax tug was tested on 2 October after an engine change at Portsmouth. During the flight it landed at Funtington Advance Landing Ground in West Sussex to test out the airfield's suitability for larger aircraft. Most Horsa testing occurred at Christchurch – on some occasions George piloted the Horsa, on others the tug. However, on 16 November he flew the Whitley to Portsmouth where he towed one of the Horsa prototypes to 6,000 feet. The following day he collected the Horsa again and delivered it to Farnborough.

George flew his Swallow to Bristol Whitchurch, via Castle Coombe, on 9 October. At Whitchurch he was given instruction by BOAC's Capt. Veasey on Curtiss CW20 *St Louis* G-AGDI. He returned again for further instruction on 23 October, including landings at Lyneham. The following day he flew the CW20 down to Hurn where it was required by Bristols for trials. After these trials George was asked to return it to Bristols at Filton on 7 January 1944, undertaking single-engine performance and general handling trials en route. The aircraft was known to be difficult to fly in such circumstances. A replacement Whitley V tug arrived at Christchurch in the middle of November and, by way of test, George flew it on five Horsa towing flights. By now there were large numbers of Horsas appearing from Christchurch that required testing. George developed a technique of landing the Horsa very close to the Halifax waiting by the flight shed in order to save time – sometimes right up to the door. Alternatively, after a test flight he would land close to the next waiting Horsa. On 10 November he undertook seven Horsa test flights from Christchurch. Then two days later he undertook seven Oxford flights from Portsmouth.

The new year of 1944 did not bring any great changes in George's test programme. He noted in his logbook that 3 January was the first occasion he had taken off on Portsmouth's south-west runway in Whitley tug EB341, towing a Horsa. Then on 17 February he noted he was able to use Christchurch's new runway whilst testing an Oxford. This had been laid by the Americans prior to the arrival of USAAF P-47s in March. Their operations caused a few problems with Horsa and Oxford testing. On 12 February, George returned to Netheravon to fly a couple of Horsas on Army loading trials. One was flown with a jeep lashed to a ski-fitted platform and another with a Bofors Gun and its ammunition. Oxford NM449 had been fitted with a modified engine intake and cowls. It was subjected to a number of extended tests, not just local flights, to test the effectiveness of the modifications. On 28 February George flew it to Netheravon, Baginton and Bristol to build up hours, followed by Netheravon, Christchurch (twice) and Cosford the following day. On 26 March, he flew a six-hour thirty-minute flight in it as far north as the Isle of Man, then south-west to Lundy before returning home. He visited Brize Norton and Cosford to fly new Horsas, also undertaking trials with them at Thorney Island. On 7 May he undertook a 'tour' in an Oxford taking in Netheravon, Broadwell, Brize Norton and Harwell before returning home, via Worthy Down. These were all RAF Horsa bases. Then there was a lull for the first few days of June – perhaps something else important was happening over the South Coast.

For a complete change George was seconded to BOAC during 1944 as an Honorary Captain for a number of route experience flights. This was to gain airline experience prior to Airspeed developing their Brabazon IIb airliner. Under the command of Captain Neil, he flew Liberator G-AGFR from Lyneham to Gibraltar late on 20 April – a flight of over six hours. Next day it was on to Castel Benito and then Cairo – a further eleven hours. After a stopover in Cairo it was back to Castel Benito and Lisbon on 24 April, with the final leg to Lyneham late on 25 April. The night-time flights over the Bay of Biscay were necessary to avoid Luftwaffe fighters. The next secondment was on 22 June with a night-time flight to Rabat under the command of Captain Dykes, again in a Liberator. As before, it was on to Castel Benito and Cairo, with George undertaking the take-off at Castel Benito. After the usual stop-over George piloted the Liberator for the return to Castel Benito on 26 June. Then on to Rabat on 27 June, a stop at St Mawgan early the next day before returning to Lyneham. The third trip with BOAC was in October, flying York G-AGJB. Under the command of Captain Rendall it departed Lyneham on 25 October for Rabat, with Castel Benito and Cairo reached the following day. The return flight commenced on 29 October making Castel Benito and Rabat, then on to Lyneham on 30 October. On this leg George handled the controls for the take-offs and landings.

George's faithful Swallow had been neglected for a while. A new C of A in April 1944 enabled him to fly it up to White Waltham on 29 April, on to Hatfield on 2 May and then home. He compared the various time he took between Portsmouth and Hatfield. The Swallow took one hour twenty-five minutes, a Hornet Moth an hour, with an Oxford only thirty-five minutes. He frequently flew the Swallow to commute to Christchurch. However, in September George decided to sell it, now having use of Airspeed's 'runabout' Hornet Moth to undertake his 'tours'. The 2 October took him to Christchurch to test fly a Horsa, staying overnight before flying to Cosford to test another Horsa, then on to Darley Moor. On 4 October he flew on to Baginton and Castle Coombe for another stop-off. Then it was on to South Cerney, Little Rissington and Netheravon before returning home to Portsmouth. Presumably he was visiting units using Oxfords. During the summer a number of Mosquito PRIVs visited Airspeed to have their engines changed to Merlin XXVs, with a number flown to Wisley after completion. Horsas were still fast rolling off the Christchurch production line, with George clearing four on 14 November, then piloting the Whitley tug to clear another four on 21 November, with six on 2 December. He had a slightly different experience at Netheravon on 29 November. George climbed aboard a Waco Hadrian glider which was then snatched into the air by a passing Dakota. He then switched aircraft and flew the Dakota as it snatched the Hadrian into the air.

December 1944 saw George return to High Post to help out Supermarine. This was on a day-to-day basis as he commuted from Portsmouth. Test flights were carried out on various Spitfire XIVs and XXIs, including a number of stability tests. Another new type for George was an Auster I where he flew Supermarine's 'runabout' on a handling session on 15 December. It was back to Airspeed at Portsmouth by Christmas, piloting Horsas on stability tests at Thorney Island on 29 December.

Loaned to de Havilland at Hatfield at the beginning of 1943, George flight-tested a number of Mosquitoes, such as this Mk IV, as well as high altitude Mk XVs.

In the spring of 1943, whilst with Supermarine at Worthy Down, George undertook further high-altitude engine testing in Spitfire Mk XIVs, including JF318.

The Supermarine S24/37 R1810 was also flown by George during his time at Worthy Down. It had variable incidence wing settings to help control its speed.

Chapter 9

Peace in Sight

Despite the end of the war now being in sight, the RAF still needed further supplies of Horsas. New Year's Day 1945 saw George fly to Christchurch where he took three Horsas up for their first flight, then towed up a further four. On 3 February George started the day in Airspeed's Whitley, undertaking three tows. He then undertook seven Horsa flights in the afternoon. 7 February saw five Whitley flights, 16 February eight Horsa flights, 20 February three landings of Horsa PF696 at Beaulieu, during deflated nose wheel tests, followed by three other Horsas at Christchurch. 8 March saw George fly up to Boscombe Down by Oxford early in the morning, before returning to Christchurch to fly the Whitley on eight Horsas towing flights. 12 March saw six Horsas tested and 22 March saw six towing flights. George was earning his keep! The last Christchurch-produced Horsa flew in April 1945.

George was soon able to get his hands on something much faster. De Havilland had arranged for Airspeed to build Mosquitoes at Christchurch on their behalf – initially FBIVs. George carried out taxiing tests of RS637 on 18 February 1946 and it was later first flown by Ron Clear. George flew it again, on light- and full-load tests, on 7 March. He flew it to Hatfield on a number of other occasions before it was handed over to the RAF at the beginning of April. George delivered the second Mosquito to the ATA at Shawbury on 6 April. In June one of the Mosquitoes played up and had to have nine check flights before George was happy with it. During the spring, George demonstrated a number of Oxfords to KLM pilots. These included 'runabout' PH191 at Christchurch, on 20 April, and both T1019 and DF483 at Hendon, on 30 April – these were both in use by BOAC as crew training aircraft.

George and Ron's glider piloting skills were called upon by Armstrong Whitworth Aircraft in the spring of 1945. The company were developing a flying wing aircraft and to build up experience they first built a scale-size glider – the AW52G – which was ready at the end of February. The glider was to provide aerodynamic information for the proposed AW52 jet-powered mail carrier. George knew how to handle gliders, so early in 1945 he was asked to convert their Chief Test Pilot – Charles Turner-Hughes – on a Horsa, prior to flying the AW52G. It was agreed that George could be loaned to Armstrong Whitworth and he flew up to Baginton in the Hornet Moth on 1 March. Here a Whitley tug was waiting, so he climbed aboard, and a number of ground towing trials were carried out with the AW52G. All went well, resulting in the first flight of thirty minutes by Charles Turner-Hughes on 2 March, with further flights during the following days.

George piloted the Whitley on further tests, prior to flying the AW52G itself for twenty minutes on 16 March, which he described as with the 'general handling of [a] prototype tailless glider'. After these successes, George gave towing instruction on the Whitley to Flt Lt Eric Franklin of Armstrong Whitworth, who went on to become Senior Test Pilot, flying the AW52 flying wing. George returned to Baginton on various occasions to pilot the Whitley tug during the trials.

On 14 July 1945, George flew across to Portsmouth by Hornet Moth for a special midday ceremony. This was to demonstrate, in front of visiting dignitaries, the final Oxford off the Portsmouth production line, followed by its official handover. An early production Oxford was also on hand for the ceremony. On 27 August, the Hornet Moth took him to Gloucester's flight test base at Moreton Vallance so that he could fly his first jet. He took a Meteor III up for an hour's general handing flight in the afternoon, before returning home. However, he made no extra comment in his logbook. His next new type was the DH Dove airliner, which he flew during a visit to Hatfield on 1 October. Instruction on prototype G-AGPJ was given to him by Geoffrey Pike, who had only just taken the Dove up for its maiden flight on 25 September.

By the end of the war George's parents were still living at Cookham near Maidenhead, though neither was in the best of health. VE Day had brought no peace for George – he spent the 8 May 'touring' around the countryside in the company's Oxford 'runabout'. He started with two return trips from Christchurch to Portsmouth in the morning, then up to Baginton, on to Ashbourne and finally back down to White Waltham. These last two calls were probably family business, with White Waltham close to Cookham. On 12 May, George's mother died, aged seventy-nine. With the family still in grief, news came that George's elder brother had died at Haslar Naval Hospital four days later. After their funeral service both were buried at Cookham Parish Cemetery. During the war, George's sister Joan had met Benjamin Hayward-Browne who was the vicar at Holy Trinity, Cookham. George recalled Benjamin driving a 1930s Humber 10 car before and during the war, usually slowly! At Easter 1946, the couple married at Holy Trinity, where the parishioners made a collection so that their vicar and his new wife could spend their honeymoon in North Africa.

At Portsmouth, the first Consul conversions of surplus Oxfords were appearing from the factory, with George flying the prototype on the afternoon of 8 February 1946. He then drove over to BOAC's base at Hurn to be the honorary co-pilot that evening on a proving flight to Johannesburg, so building up further route experience. This was by York, which departed for the five-hour flight to Malta under the command of Capt. Alderson. From Malta, it was on to Cairo the following morning, Khartoum in the afternoon and on to Nairobi overnight. The morning of 10 February saw an early start for the final sector to Johannesburg, followed by a five-night stopover. The return flight started early on 15 February, retracing its steps to Nairobi, Khartoum and Cairo. Here George switched to a BOAC Lancastrian for the return to Hurn.

George wasn't happy with the performance of Christchurch-produced Mosquito RS718, so he flew it up to Supermarines at High Post on 26 August 1946. Here it was checked over by the resident Rolls-Royce representative, which included taking him up on a short flight. Although nothing definite could be found, George was still not happy with the performance of the Merlins. So, after check flight number eleven, he decided to take it up to Hatfield, where modified fuel switches were tested, on 27 September. Whilst there he bumped into Geoffrey de Havilland and John Cunningham as they were both flying that day. In the early evening, Geoffrey was killed whilst testing a DH108 Swallow prototype over the River Thames – a great loss to de Havilland. Following the death of Geoffrey, Sir Geoffrey de Havilland, his father, asked John Cunningham to take over as Chief Test Pilot. He was well known following his wartime Mosquito exploits, having rejoined de Havilland in December 1945. George undertook two more check flights on the Mosquito at Christchurch before finally releasing the aircraft to the RAF on 3 October. For their 1946 Battle of Britain Display on 14 September, George flew a Mosquito across to RAF Holmsley South where the weather was foul. A few days later George received a letter from the Station Commander:

> Just a line to thank you for your help on Saturday. We are all most grateful for what you did and, I can assure you, it was quite the most outstanding affair of the day, in spite of the gyrations of the helicopter, as everyone was most impressed by the way you handled the Mosquito when practically every other living being, including those specially designed for flying, had taken to their feet.

George's logbook contained no comment as to the adverse weather. Later, George had a problem during another test flight:

> During a dive down to sea level at a big pace for those days, a seagull butted up against the starboard wing of the Mosquito. It is a strongly made wing, but the gull went through the leading edge, then right through the front spar, down the wing and through the front webb of the rear spar, and then gave up from sheer exhaustion. It requires a strong constitution to stand that sort of thing.

As well as a Whitley, Airspeed at Christchurch were provided with an early Halifax as a Horsa tug. George (centre, dark overalls) and his team pose for the camera.

There were changes with George's contact at *The Aeroplane*. Thurston James had been appointed editor in December 1945, but still sought information from George. Peter Masefield had moved on to the Ministry of Civil Aviation. Still to come in 1949 was his appointment as Chief Executive of BEA. In due course, George would have plenty of dealings with him in his new capacity.

The AW52G flying wing glider RG324 at Baginton, in March 1945. George is amongst the bystanders offering advice to the test crew.

George prepares to pass on his knowledge to Charles Turner-Hughes – the AW52G Chief Test Pilot – concerning glider flight characteristics.

A special event was held at Portsmouth in July 1945 to mark delivery of the final Oxford. George is in front of the port engine, with Ron Clear to his left.

At the end of the war the Christchurch factory started producing Mosquitoes – this is a B35 late in 1947. Now outdated, very few saw service.

Above left and right: George (left) and Ron Clear (right) with Christchurch-built Mosquitoes.

Chapter 10

Ambassador

Airspeed's design for a new airliner to meet the Brabazon Committee requirements for a Dakota replacement was accepted by the MAP, who ordered two prototypes. Advance planning was undertaken and in 1946 George was selected as the aircraft's test pilot, now spending much of his time at Christchurch. Airspeed acquired a surplus Warwick bomber in order to flight test the Centaurus engines proposed for the Ambassador. George visited Vickers's Flight Test Base at Wisley on 11 April, where he was given brief instruction on a Warwick by Wing Cdr George Lowdell, followed by a general handing flight around Surrey. On 24 April he flew up to Filton where he collected Warwick HG341, which was the aircraft to be used by Airspeed. Flown again on 3 May on Centaurus installation trials, similar flights were carried out over the next few days. Engine power and consumption trials commenced on 16 May, usually of one hour and thirty minutes duration. Normally these would be in the Christchurch locality, although South Marston, Woodsbridge and Beaulieu were all visited. By the autumn intensive cruising tests of up to three hours long were being undertaken.

George visited Miles Aircraft at Woodley early in June 1946. Pre-war he had test flown the Alvis Leonides engine in the Bulldog, and production was now getting underway. To update the pre-war testing an Oxford was re-engined by Miles with two 515 hp Leonides engines and first flown from Woodley, on behalf of Alvis, on 3 June. There were indications of vibration and tail buffeting, which George was asked to report on. He found the new engines gave the Oxford a hasty turn of speed. Whilst there he also undertook a short flight in Oxford U7 fitted with a 'Miles Electric Co-pilot', which was the company's early efforts to develop an automatic pilot.

The 1 January 1947 saw George flying up to Hatfield where he had a quick flight in Vampire FI TG/285 – his second jet fighter. He also discussed Horsa flying with John Cunningham, whom he noted in his diary as 'Group Captain'. As part of the development of the Comet jet airliner, a surplus Horsa had been modified to have a Comet nose shape fitted. This was to be flown by John, after instruction from George. As the Hatfield runway was being resurfaced, they met up at Radlett on 2 January to undertake the first instruction flight, with another the following day. In due course the Horsa moved across to Hatfield for Cunningham to assess the pilot's view, especially during rainstorms. George returned home from Radlett in the Hornet Moth, but bad weather and strong winds forced him to land at Eastleigh to refuel before making it back to Christchurch. On another visit to Hatfield on 15 May, George undertook general flying on the new

Chipmunk prototype. This Canadian-designed trainer had arrived at Hatfield in January and was later produced in large numbers for the RAF.

By the beginning of 1947 the prototype Ambassador G-AGUA was beginning to take shape in the Experimental Hangar at Christchurch. George and the other pilots kept an eye on its progress, as well as liaising with Arthur Hagg, who was Airspeed's Chief Designer. Engine testing continued with the Warwick, which had an overhaul at the beginning of May. Single-engine performance trials were undertaken in June, with one of the engines failing on take-off tests at Boscombe Down. By then G-AGUA was complete and it was rolled out of the hangar at the end of the month. George undertook the first engine runs and taxiing trials on 30 June, followed by a short hop on 1 July. Further ground hops were undertaken on 8 July to fully get the feel of the new airliner, with further ones on the morning of 10 July. Finally, George was happy with everything and took the Ambassador on its fifty-minute maiden flight later in the afternoon, accompanied by John Pears as his flight observer and engineer. The press reported George as saying 'the aircraft behaved well'. However, the truth was that the flight was a nightmare for both pilots. Shortly after take-off the central rudder's spring-tab broke, setting up severe vibration of the tail assembly. Luckily this stopped after thirty seconds when the spring tab broke away. The elevators then set themselves in the fully down position with George and John hauling on their control columns to bring the aircraft's nose back up. Eventually the problem resolved itself and the aircraft returned to a happier position. Worse was to follow, as set out in George's report on:

> The very commendable behaviour of Pears under conditions of stress and extreme tension. Shortly after take-off there was every indication that the aircraft might either get out of control or break up. Not more than four minutes later both electric and hydraulic systems failed completely. Pears acted quietly and efficiently attending to instructions immediately, changing fuses and operating relays with discernment and initiative, with the eventual recovery of both hydraulic and electric services thus enabling a landing to be made. Had it not been for this exemplary behaviour, the conditions for the pilot would have been worsened and the aircraft would have made an emergency landing at Holmsley with the risk of damage as most services were not available.

George made one of his full reports to Arthur Hagg – the Ambassador's designer – which resulted in John receiving a £10 cheque by way of Airspeed's thanks for his coolness during the flight. After all this 'excitement' it was back into the hangar for adjustment, prior to its second flight on 22 August.

Thinking such problems were behind them, George and John flew most days to build up hours, including an appearance over Christchurch Regatta on 23 August. It was then time to prepare for the annual SBAC flying display, but aileron control was posing a major concern. George was worried about the problem, with the Airspeed directors anxious for the Ambassador to build up the necessary ten hours' flying to make it eligible to appear at the show. Having achieved this, a limited twenty-minute flying display was devised by George, with John concentrating on the errant ailerons. George flew the Ambassador to Radlett on 7 September and brief, but polished, flying demonstrations were given on the three days of the show (9–11 Sept). However, George kept the aircraft close to the airfield should an emergency arise. There were none and praise for the display was received from the aeronautical press as well as the Airspeed directors. On 14 September, George demonstrated the prototype at the RAeS garden party, also held at Radlett, and, on 15 September, he flew it up to Hatfield. Here it was checked over by the DH test pilots, led by John Cunningham. Then back to Christchurch in the evening to continue test flying, including sorting problems with the undercarriage, fins and rudders.

Ron Clear first flew G-AGUA as first pilot on 21 September 1947, becoming the Ambassador Development Test Pilot. He undertook much time on perfecting the flight control systems. Further trials continued throughout the autumn – 'an exemplary aircraft and easy to fly'. On 25 September, George flew the Ambassador up to Brize Norton where there was a small demonstration of aircraft to the Armed Services, including a Bristol Freighter and Vickers Viking. However, the main reason for the visit was to see the USAAF C-54 Skymaster, which had just flown across the North Atlantic under radio control. Shortly after taking off to return home, the front crew door of the Ambassador flew open due to not having been correctly shut. George feathered the starboard engine and made an emergency landing at Thruxton. The door was tied up and the Ambassador returned safely to Christchurch. Further problems occurred during a flight over the English Channel on the afternoon of 21 November when the starboard undercarriage leg dropped down following a bolt failure. Due to the speed of the aircraft, the strain deflected the starboard wing, resulting in a rapid climbing roll to starboard. Luckily the wing remained attached. On this occasion, John's comments:

> When cruising at around 260 knots the starboard undercarriage tore away and crashed rearwards, together with all the hydraulic piping and bits and pieces from the wheel well. This caused the starboard wing to deflect, giving a negative incidence relative to the remainder of the aircraft and causing a rapid climbing roll to starboard. The noise of the undercarriage coming down was like a six inch shell exploding. I was moved rapidly from the second pilot's seat to a position round George's neck, from which attitude I struggled to remove myself and contribute something useful to the situation. Comparing notes afterwards we thought the wing had sheared off. After George had the aircraft on an even keel, I went aft and found the undercarriage trailing, with hydraulic fluid streaming along the engine nacelle. We called base and asked for advice whether to land with the remaining undercarriage up or down. We were told to land with them down, which we did.

Having orbited for two hours, George landed gingerly but safely, with the limp starboard wheel folding up and the aircraft swerving off the runway when its nose-wheel tyres burst, luckily with little damage. Repairs to the errant locking mechanism were quickly completed but it was felt further modifications should be made. George took the Ambassador up for a quick ten-minute flight on 13 December to check the undercarriage retraction sequence. Then it was off on a more normal three-hour test flight. It was during all this testing that George's aeronautical engineering skills came to the fore. Prior to each flight he would be given detailed instructions by the engineering team as to what task he was to undertake. On return he would normally have carried out the required task, but he would then discuss with them what he felt about the flight and how any problem might be solved. He also provided them with a very detailed report of each flight. This was how he became part of the team, not just the Chief Test Pilot. John Pears grew to call him 'Uncle George'. In December 1947, under some pressure from the Ministry of Supply, BEA announced that it would require twenty Ambassadors, although it was some months before the formal order was signed. This resulted in a demonstration to BEA Officials in the spring of 1948, and on 10 March to Group Capt. Christopher Clarkson – the British Civil Air Attaché to the United States.

George received further 'heavy' aircraft experience in December 1947 when he flew as a passenger in a Qantas L.749 Constellation, commenting that he was 'privileged to fly the world's best commercial airliner'. He produced his usual detailed report for Airspeed on its performance with a final comment:

> The greatest risk to life and limb appeared to be during the descent of the wet, steep and very slippery staircase after the flight.

Then, in March 1948, George flew across the Atlantic aboard a BOAC Constellation. On 15 March he flew as second pilot under the command of Capt. Nesbit on the short first stage of the flight to Shannon, where the passengers disembarked for dinner. After refuelling it was then into the twelve hours, night-time 2,000-mile sector to Gander. After a break the flight continued to New York La Guardia, now under the command of Capt. Bullock. Later in the evening the aircraft returned to Montreal, where George stopped off. On 19 October he undertook a two-hour thirty-minute general assessment of the Constellation under the instruction of Capt. Pentland, prior to returning to New York. George departed New York on 25 March under the command of Capt. Woodman for the eleven-hour thirty-minute, 3,300-mile haul to Shannon. Here they refuelled before returning to Heathrow. George used the name Heathrow as it was not until the 1950s that the London Airport title came into fashion. Airspeed was provided with his usual report on 'a very fine aircraft – justifies the high opinion of pilots'. During his stay in New York, George had visited the Glenn Martin Company at Baltimore to look over their Martin 202, which was a similar size to the Ambassador. Unfortunately, the weather was too bad to undertake a demonstration flight, but George was given a detailed look around the 202. He had already noted that he needed to inspect the aircraft's double-slotted flaps – a must for George. An aside to his US visit was the 'problem' George had with a passenger when returning home. A lady seated in front of him had a clear view of the engines as they took off from New York in the dark. At full power there were 2-foot flames emitted from them leading to red-hot exhaust pipes. An unseasoned traveller, she jumped up and asked George if the aircraft was on fire. He explained that the effect was quite normal, though not noticeable on daylight flights. After a long talk she became content that the Constellation was not going to blow up and, in due course, was able to sleep for the rest of the journey. On arrival at Heathrow she told the captain that if she had not been so adequately assured by George, she might have had a fit.

The Ambassador prototype G-AGUA was rolled out from the Christchurch factory in June 1947. Onlookers soon appeared during initial engine runs.

The unpainted Ambassador prototype outside the Christchurch hangars in June 1947. Again, there is a crowd of onlookers from the factory.

Annotated photo of the Ambassador departing on its maiden flight on the evening of 10 July 1947. The flight didn't prove straightforward.

George setting the controls of an Ambassador prototype, prior to another test flight.

George and John Pears after the maiden flight.

Arthur Hagg (designer) with George.

Ron Clear and John Pears undertook much test flying.

George after the maiden flight.

The Ambassador design team – Arthur Hagg and George Miles – at Christchurch in 1948.

George demonstrating prototype G-AGUA at the SBAC Radlett Show in September 1947, receiving praise from the aeronautical press.

Vickers Warwick HG341 was used by Airspeed at Christchurch as an engine test bed for the Bristol Centaurus engines used by the Ambassador.

The first of a number of Ambassador 'heavy' landings, this one being at Christchurch on 21 November 1947. G-AGUA was soon back in the air.

The Portsmouth factory converted many Oxfords into Consul airliners. Among these was MC-ABA, which was flown by George in November 1946.

George undertook transatlantic travel to New York in March 1948 courtesy of BOAC Constellations. On some of the flights he acted as second pilot.

Chapter 11

De Havilland on the Scene

In May 1948, de Havilland Aircraft completed its financial acquisition of Airspeed. However, the Airspeed name continued in use for a further three years. Arthur Hagg left the company, becoming a consultant for Sir Alan Cobham at Flight Refuelling. Arthur's place as Chief Designer was taken by George Miles, who arrived from Miles Aircraft. George was already acquainted with him from his visits to the Miles factory. In April 1949, Major Hereward de Havilland was appointed to the Board. He was the younger brother of Sir Geoffrey de Havilland.

At the time the prototype Ambassador was having various modifications incorporated. During the period, George managed to try out a few new types. On 28 May he flew an assessment of the flight characteristics of Vickers Viking VW214; on 9 June a general assessment of Goodyear Duck amphibian NC5506M (fitted with a self-castoring undercarriage); on 24 June Saab Safir SE-BFU at Gatwick, during the RAC International Rally; on 9 July a visit to Farnborough to fly a Fortress under command of Flt Lt Martin to investigate its ailerons; on 10 August a Tudor II at Boscombe Down under command of Group Capt. Purvis, undertaking full-load handling assessment. On 23 August, George was invited to fly the Saab Scandia prototype SE-BCA at Christchurch, this being Saab's response to a Dakota replacement. The Scandia was on a UK demonstration tour, under command of Capt. Claes Smith, Saab's Chief Test Pilot.

Ambassador testing commenced again on 8 June with taxiing trials and three ground hops undertaken by George at Christchurch. Satisfied all was in order, he set off on an hour's flight. Testing continued throughout the summer to check vibration, aileron and flap settings and rudder modifications, with George first recording Ron Clear as his second pilot on 16 June. After one flight, where George experienced severe tail vibration, it was found that most of the bolts had broken and fallen out! George and John flew G-AGUA to Portsmouth on 17 June so the Airspeed employees could have a close-up look at the new airliner. George undertook a beat-up of the airfield on arrival, the Ambassador being the largest aircraft ever to land at Portsmouth. On 6 July, George undertook a demonstration for Geoffrey Pike of DH Propellers as there was some concern over the propeller's governing mechanism. This was examined by representatives from DH, resulting in a replacement port propeller with strain gauges being fitted. On 16 August, George successfully completed a single-engine take-off from Christchurch, something he would perfect by the next month. On 30 August, the prototype undertook a number of aileron flutter tests at varying heights. This involved diving the aircraft at full speed before pulling up. For a while all went well. When pulling out at 2,000 feet over the airfield severe flutter developed, which set up resonance throughout the aircraft. Although only lasting around twenty seconds, everything was a blur for George and John as, once again, they fought to maintain control. On landing they both inspected the ailerons. On opening the port aileron shroud, John found both centre hinges were fractured. He found the same with the starboard hinges. George's comment was, 'Well John, we were nearly a short paragraph in the local paper.'

Meanwhile, the second Ambassador prototype G-AKRD, fitted with a pressurised fuselage, had been completed and George undertook its first taxiing trials on 19 August. These had to be curtailed due to problems with the brakes, delaying the first flight on 26 August. On its third day of flying – 3 September – George flew the Ambassador to Beaulieu, where he undertook a single-engine take-off and flight assessment in preparation for the forthcoming SBAC show at Farnborough. George's first demonstration at the show was on 7 September, but on the third day he amazed everyone by flying the entire display on the starboard engine only. He lined up for take-off, shut down the port engine, took-off, did his display, landed again and restarted the port engine. This was the first such demonstration in public – and only George's third time! The demonstration confounded the protagonists of four engine airliners who insisted twins were unsafe. On 20 September BEA finally signed its £3 million order for twenty Ambassadors, with G-AGUA having been demonstrated to the airline at Northolt, on 22 July. At the time, the airline favoured a proven piston engine formula over an unproven turboprop used in the Viscount. The order was looked on with gloom by Vickers-Armstrongs who had hoped their Viscount would have been ordered by BEA. It finally was in August 1950.

For the remainder of 1948 the majority of George's flying time was spent testing G-AGUA. At the beginning of October, familiarisation flights were undertaken at Christchurch with various BEA captains. Then, on 14 October, the Ambassador was flown to Hatfield for a demonstration flight to de Havilland VIPs, including Sir Geoffrey, followed by a further inspection by BEA VIPs at Northolt. This was in connection with the thirtieth anniversary of regular London to Paris air services. In the middle of November, overload take-offs were undertaken by George and Ron with G-AGUA at Beaulieu – the maximum weight building up to 52,000 pounds. Sandbags and water ballast were used to slowly increase the aircraft's weight, but even so George still managed to take off in half the runway's length. G-AKRD could not be used as its wing structure was not strong enough and it did not have water jettison capabilities. It was later discovered by the Structures Department that G-AGUA's wing was not stressed for these take-off weights either! At the end of the month, George undertook some flights as Hon. Captain in BEA Vikings in order to gain experience of the operating condition the Ambassador would expect. This involved trips from Northolt to Marseilles, Rome, Athens and Istanbul. During December 1948 and January 1949, G-AKRD was flown in conjunction with Capt. 'Dickie' Rymer of BEA and a Boscombe Down pilot. This included flying at Christchurch, Beaulieu, Chilbolton and Boscombe Down and mainly concerned engine performance on take-off and landings.

George flew Ambassador G-AKRD up to Hatfield on 12 January 1949 for a fuller demonstration for John Cunningham. Whilst there, it was flown by two of their test pilots – John Derry and Geoffrey Pike. Flying with both prototypes continued throughout the spring. G-AGUA had been in the hangars having its nose-wheel mounting modified.

It was involved in shimmy tests at Beaulieu and was delivered to Boscombe Down on 22 February for assessment under Lt Com. Stuart of the Civil Aircraft Testing Section. Measurements of its single-engine performance and stalling speeds were carried out. However, the pilots considered the Ambassador's single-engine climbing performance as to be so poor that airworthiness requirements could not be met. Presumably they had not seen George's Farnborough demonstration. Whilst taxiing in from a flight on 10 March, G-AGUA's brakes failed and it collided with two parked Tiger Moths. Gp Capt. H. A. Purvis was partially blamed for taxiing too fast, the aircraft returning to Christchurch for patching up. On 2 May, night flying was undertaken with G-AKRD at Hurn with BEA's Captains James and Rymes. This was for them to check the window screen optics at night. However, there were still continuing problems with the fins and rudders. G-AGUA had its central fin and rudder removed at the end of June and was flown as such on 4 July. This did not cure the problem and so the fin and rudder were refitted. G-AKRD had the new Decca Navigation Flight Plotter installed and George approved of this new navigation equipment. Originally produced during the war for marine use, it was developed by Decca for aviation, with the prototype units literally being road tested. Airspeed then agreed to install it in the Ambassador for further trials, which proved successful. George was able to rely on the Flight Plotter as many of his flights were above cloud and so he could not see the ground to check his position.

1949 saw George re-experience some of his wartime testing at Christchurch. Airspeed rebuilt a number of Horsas during 1948/49, on behalf of the RAF. He had to test some of these and deliver them to Wroughton by piloting the Halifax tug. On 31 May, George set off from Christchurch in the Halifax, towing Ron in a Horsa. Following take-off, the Horsa's wheels fell off into an adjacent garden and so the flight was cut short. George towed the Horsa round for a successful landing on its skid. The crews then went over to the Mudeford side of the airfield where the wheels had dropped. An irate gardener greeted them showing a great hole where his sweet peas should have been. He seemed oblivious that the wheels had bounced into an adjacent garden where a group of children had gathered to have their photograph taken. The event was not recorded on camera. The gardener wrote to Airspeed complaining that:

> Your big four engined aircraft towing an equally large glider continues to trespass on my property by passing over at very low altitude, much below the right of air to a freeholder. This letter is to notify you that I, or my executors, hold you responsible for anything causing damage to life and property.

This was backed up by a letter from the Town Clerk of Christchurch concerning the incident. The end of 1949 saw a number of Horsas cleared at Christchurch as the rebuilds were coming to an end. On 16 November, George test flew four; on 30 November, three; and on 1 December, he flew the Halifax tug twice to Wroughton to deliver the gliders.

In order to build up Airspeed's knowledge of other airliners George visited KLM at Schiphol in March 1949, where a Convair 240 was demonstrated to him. This was so that he could get the feel of the American 'competition' to the Ambassador. He had two flights as a passenger, managing a brief spell in the cockpit on one of them. The flights showed the cabin pressurisation system and ILS system to advantage. George gave his usual detailed report, commenting that the Convair was a good aircraft which found high favour with KLM pilots. BEA's Capt. Rymes was invited by Vickers to undertake a flight in their new Viscount during March. During the pre-flight lunch, the Vickers' directors questioned him intensely about his experience of the Ambassador. Similarly, Capt. Rymes tried to find out as much as he could about the Viscount, reporting his findings back to George. He felt that the cockpit layout was not as simple as the Ambassador, the steering was inferior, and the elevators had undesirable characteristics. On the plus side it was very smooth and quiet in flight, and the ailerons were the best he had experienced. George received a two-hour demonstration on one of BOAC's new Argonauts at Hurn on 14 June, under the command of Capt. Holden. George's report noted that 'BOAC pilots happy'.

During the Farnborough Flying Display on 10 and 11 September, George and Ron flew G-AKRD as part of a 'heavy circus' of airliners. Afterwards they were pleased to hear a number of comments on how quiet the Ambassador was as it flew past. This was down to George's technique of flying at the quietest cruising speed and RPM, whereas pilots of the other aircraft had full-throttle, maximum cruising RPM and arrived from a dive to get maximum speed. On landing, George selected reverse pitch on both propellers, which enabled the Ambassador to slowly reverse off the runway. During the show he expanded his airliner knowledge by hitching a ride on three of them – the Viscount, Apollo and Hermes 5. He found the Viscount smooth and quiet – an improvement over the Ambassador. There was noticeable floor vibration in the cockpit and front cabin areas, but this lessened towards the rear of the cabin. George noted that the Viscount deserved the popularity that it was currently receiving. George considered the Apollo inferior, with propeller vibration noticeable in the cabin. Its pilot expressed concern with the rudder control and nose wheel steering. The Hermes 5 was the largest of the airliners, George spent his time in the right-hand pilot's seat, alongside George Hazelden. A proper assessment could not be made as Hazelden was flying the aircraft to its limits – not normal airline fashion. As usual, George made his detailed report back to the Airspeed directors. George demonstrated G-AKRD to BEA VIPs, including their recently appointed new Chief Executive, his long-term friend, Peter Masefield, at Christchurch on 10 October 1949. The *Bournemouth Echo* reported the VIPs as saying, 'Most impressed. One of the world's best airliners.' At Christchurch the pilot's office was situated on the first floor and was reached by an external wooden staircase. There was a telephone by the door and George recalls its 'code'. One ring meant he was needed on the airfield; two rings was to call him to the boss; three rings meant he had been sacked! The 'code' system varied depending on who George was recounting the story to!

There was not so much light aircraft flying for George compared to pre-war days. The members of South Hants Ultra Light Aircraft Club at Christchurch had built Heath Parasol ultra-light G-AJCK during 1948. In the spring of 1949, they asked George to undertake its first flight, but it proved to be underpowered and would not leave the ground, so it was back into the hangar (it was later re-engined and flown from Hurn). George's former Comper Swift G-ACTF had now been acquired by Ron Clear and was kept in the Flight Shed. George was able to reacquaint himself with it with a flight on 12 August. On 6 October he had a brief flight in a Zaunkoenig ultra light, which was visiting the South Hants ULAC rally at Christchurch, with a demonstration by one of the Club pilots described as 'sensational'. Ron took part with his Swift.

Above and below: In November 1948, visits were made to Beaulieu by G-AGUA for measured take-off trials on their hard runway – Christchurch was still grass at the time.

Attracting attention is Goodyear Duck amphibian NC5506M, which visited Christchurch in June 1948. George flew it for 'a general assessment'.

Sweden's idea of a Dakota replacement, Saab Scandia SE-BCA, visited Christchurch two months later in August to enable the Airspeed test pilots to assess its handling.

George would frequently fly Airspeed's resident Halifax tug RT935 during 1948/49 in connection with the Horsa overhaul contract.

After they had been overhauled, George found himself resuming Horsa testing at Christchurch during 1948/49. At the time the RAF still considered there was a need for gliders.

Both George and Ron tried to fly this locally built Heath Parasol at Christchurch in 1949 – both failed. Re-engining later proved the answer.

Chapter 12

Trials (and Tribulations) and De Havilland Takeover

Further airliner familiarisation took George to Filton on 16 February 1950, where he flew as a passenger on a BOAC Stratocruiser. He then received instruction from Capt. May, who was in charge of BOAC's pilot training and an old acquaintance. George's resulting report concluded that the Stratocruiser was 'the most complicated piece of flying machinery I know to date'. He noted BOAC's low utilisation of the type – less than three hours per day – whereas BEA was anticipating eight hours for the Ambassador and Viscount. Whilst flying G-AGUA on 17 February, George called at Hatfield where he was given co-pilot experience on the Comet prototype by John Cunningham. Although both Chief Test Pilots of their respective companies, their working relationship was rather frosty. John was of the old school where pilots did their job but didn't mix with the engineers, whereas George had always sought their opinions. On another visit to Hatfield in July, George was given an assessment flight on the Heron prototype by Geoffrey Pike, who had only just taken the Heron up for its maiden flight a couple of months earlier. The Christchurch factory became involved in the development of the de Havilland Vampire Trainer, which was taken up for its maiden flight on 15 November by John Wilson – one of the Hatfield test pilots. John had come to Christchurch to undertake the flight due to his experience of testing the similar Vampire Night Fighter. It would appear that George's only involvement was to fly a Fairchild Argus over to Hurn in the afternoon to collect John after his flight. George did get his hands on a trials Vampire FB5 for general assessment on 14 December on an attempted flight from Christchurch to Hatfield, but this appears to have ended up at Farnborough.

Having obtained BEA's order for the Ambassador, Airspeed was now looking for further orders. Aer Lingus showed interest and a demonstration was arranged for them in January 1950. George and John departed Christchurch in G-AKRD on 22 January, cleared customs at Hurn and flew on to Dublin Collinstown Airport. George let the new Decca Navigation do the hard work of guiding them there. The following two days were taken up with demonstration flights to Aer Lingus aircrew and technicians, also taking in Shannon, but no order was forthcoming. G-AKRD returned to Hurn for braking tests where it suffered an accident on 13 March. On take-off George cut one engine, with the Ambassador failing to gain height as anticipated and sinking back onto the runway. Emergency crews were quickly on the scene and there was minimal damage to the fuselage. George commented to the press, 'It is one of those unfortunate mishaps which must be expected when engaged on extensive testing work.' Temporary repairs were carried out to enable the aircraft to be flown back to Christchurch for full repairs.

George drove back to Hurn on 3 May as there had been a similar accident – this time to a BOAC Hermes IV. Whilst crew training, it was landing with one engine out. The pilot attempted to go around again, opening up the engines and retracting the undercarriage, but, like the Ambassador, the Hermes sank onto the runway with its propellers digging into the tarmac. George wanted to compare the damage sustained by the Ambassador with that to the low-winged Hermes. He found that the underside of the fuselage was not touched, the weight of the aircraft being taken by the engine nacelles and partly retracted undercarriage doors. George reported that the Hermes could not be moved as easily as the Ambassador, although he felt repairs to the engines would be completed quicker than repairs to the Ambassador's fuselage. At the time of his report the third Ambassador prototype G-ALFR was nearing completion. George undertook initial taxiing trials early on 18 May, followed by a short hop, prior to its first flight later in the day. G-AKRD rejoined the flight test programme a few days later and George spent the summer flying all three prototypes, sharing the flying with Ron Clear. Also joining the team was Brian Powell, who had been a test pilot for Vickers-Armstrongs. George completed 108 stalls in one day whilst flying G-AKRD with C of G being changed throughout the testing. George commenced testing at 14,000 feet and slowly descended to 1,500 feet. Then, G-ALFR suffered an accident on 12 July whilst on test from Hurn. Landing at high weight, with three green lights showing, the starboard undercarriage folded up due to a latch failure. The resulting slide down the runway again resulted in minor damage to the fuselage and a sense of déjà vu for George.

Demonstrations to prospective customers continued during 1950, with G-AKRD assessed at Christchurch by Reg Butler, of Australia's Butlers Air Transport, on 21 June. At the Farnborough Show at the beginning of September it flew as part of an airliner 'circus', not an individual demonstration. George flew it in company with the likes of the Tay-Viscount and Varsity. It was demonstrated to RAF Transport Command Brass on 20 September and 8 December, to Capt. Mallard of Malayan Airways in September and Alitalia officials the following month. G-ALFR gained fame on 13 November whilst being flown by Ron Clear. At overload weight and with C of G well aft it landed heavily at Christchurch after Ron had tried to initiate a go around. Such was the force of the Ambassador hitting the ground that both engines broke clean away from their mountings. On hearing the news, George rushed from home expecting the worse but was surprised to find there was little damage, so he took to the air in the Argus to take photos of the scene. As a memento of the incident, George sent Ron a nautical-themed cartoon marked 'finished with engines'. The crash also cured the co-pilot's back pains. The aircraft returned to the air on 12 January 1951 and was soon involved in de-icing trials over the North Sea. George flew G-ALFR to Hatfield on 5 April for measured take-off and landing tests at maximum 52,500 lb weight. One accelerated landing stop resulted in the port undercarriage tyre bursting. On the final scheduled single-engine test, the starboard engine caught fire. This was soon extinguished with George making a safe one-engine landing, the crew returning to Christchurch in a Consul.

In BEA's September 1950 magazine Peter Masefield, now the Airline's Chief Executive, commented, 'The most famous era in British history was the Elizabethan era – and may be again one day.' Then, in November, the airline announced the results of a staff competition to select new class names for its new fleet of airliners. The Ambassador would be known as the Elizabethan Class and the Viscount as the Discovery Class. The name was nothing to do with Queen Elizabeth II as she did not become Queen until February 1952. BEA used the Elizabethan name to promote their new airliner – hence many passengers did not realise they were flying in an Ambassador. BEA said they wanted a competitive name to make their aircraft distinct from those of other airlines. On the other hand, the Viscount was publicised as the Discovery Class, but this name did not catch on with travellers. BEA's first production aircraft – G-AMAD – was flown by Ron on 12 January 1951. This aircraft had been switched with the first of BEA's batch – G-ALZN (flown 10 April) – for publicity purposes as the registration represented AMbassADor. However, BEA's Chairman, Peter Masefield, said that G-AMAD was named *Sir Francis Drake* to tie in with Admiral Drake. Similarly, G-ALZN was named *Elizabethan* to tie in with its registration and, during September, BEA used it for trials on their Northolt to Paris Le Bourget services.

Major changes came to the Portsmouth and Christchurch sites in June 1951 when the Airspeed name disappeared from the factories, which now carried de Havilland Aircraft titles on their façades. They were now the Airspeed Division of de Havilland. Following the takeover, all test and development flying at Christchurch came under the jurisdiction of John Cunningham at Hatfield. As the local Chief Test Pilot, George continued test flying the Ambassadors, with G-AKRD loaned to BEA for crew training. He had the honour to hand over the 'ships papers' of G-ALZN *Elizabethan* to Capt. Charles Riley – Flight Captain of BEA's Elizabethan Flight – at Heathrow on the morning of 22 August 1951. It was soon joined by G-AMAD, but both soon had to be returned to Airspeed for latest modifications. Prior to delivery, G-AMAD had suffered a familiar accident at Christchurch on 17 June when piloted by Brian Powell, with BEA Training Captains and Crews on board. On landing, the main starboard undercarriage leg failed, but there was little damage during the resulting skid along the grass. Again, repairs did not take long. Final icing trials were undertaken during the winter of 1951/52, which involved BEA crews in G-AMAD who didn't have much luck in finding ice. G-ALFR was flown up to Heathrow in December 1951, from where George and BEA crews flew to Copenhagen Kastrup in January 1952, searching for cumulus nimbus clouds. On 13 January the aircraft was struck by lightning, resulting in both wind screens cracking and the wireless set blowing up. On checking the aircraft at Kastrup, it was found to be fully magnetised, which necessitated George flying it back to Farnborough in order to be de-magnetised. George finally found suitable icing conditions over the English Channel and Brittany on 23 January, with a follow-up trip three weeks later. On another occasion, George was flying G-ALFR over Somerset on load trials with a test crew of seven. Stalls at height were being undertaken when a loud crack was heard from the rear of the aircraft. The flight engineer walked through the fuselage but could see nothing amiss, so he went through the bulkhead to check the rear fuselage area. Here he found one of the tailplane attachment bolts had broken, leaving just one to hold the tailplane on. Fearing the worst, the test crew prepared to take to their parachutes, but George managed to calm them down, gingerly returning to Christchurch. On examination it was found that the remaining bolt would have broken within a few minutes!

On 24 September 1951 George gave demonstrations to the directors of Trans-Australia Airlines and aviation officials from Southern Rhodesia. TAA showed interest, as had Australia National Airways, so a sales team was dispatched to Australia. In November the Editor of the *Christchurch Times* ran a headline item on Airspeed and the Ambassador. This was to counter some of the negative press that he felt the Ambassador was receiving and to view the company's future under de Havilland. De Havilland said that the Ambassador's future depended on government policy – whether it supported production of civil aircraft or the development of military types. They were quoting an Ambassador delivery time of twenty-one months at an increased price of £225,000. Then came a bombshell. In December 1951 de Havilland announced that it would no longer proceed with the Ambassador, calling off sales negotiations with TAA, ANA and Central African Airways, leaving just the twenty aircraft for BEA. De Havilland felt that it would be too costly to bring the Ambassador to international standard and that it needed to spend development money elsewhere. Initially this did not have a great effect on George as he continued with production flight testing of the remaining BEA aircraft. However, de Havilland gradually utilised the Christchurch factory for jet fighter production – initially this was Vampire Trainers for the RAF and RN, followed by export orders. The first production Vampire T11 had been flown by Geoffrey Pike in January 1952, with later testing undertaken by John Derry and John Wilson, both normally based at Hatfield. The Vampires were followed by Venoms for the RAF and Sea Venoms for the Navy, with George continuing to be involved in their flight testing. On one occasion he undertook eleven tests in two days. There was still some Ambassadors flying at Christchurch as a number of the early production aircraft were brought up to full airline standard. George was in contact with Thurstan James of *The Aeroplane*. In March 1953 he wrote:

> Fairly busy with Ambassador testing. I find I am scurrying round the sky in these blow-lamps a good deal, even at my great age. Grandpa finds the pure jet does not rattle his dentures like the old piston engine.

The changes at Christchurch saw the departure of many of George's friends and colleagues. Ron Clear moved to the Chester factory, eventually becoming Airfield Manager at Hatfield; John Pears returned to Vickers-Armstrongs; George Miles left early in 1952 to rejoin the family firm at Shoreham.

George flew G-AMAB to Hatfield on 14 June 1953 to take part in the Royal Aeronautical Society's garden party marking fifty years of flying. As is often the case at these events, the weather was not kind, so George made a low fly-past, in fact standing in for a demonstration by USAF F-86 Sabres which couldn't find the airfield due to the low cloud. George kept in contact with a number of his Airspeed colleagues, updating them on the Ambassador's entry into service. He wrote to George Miles concerning a flight to Milan in September 1953 at the invitation of BEA. He learnt that Sir Winston Churchill had recently flown to Nice by BEA Viscount. For some reason Churchill took a dislike to the aircraft and advised BEA that he would only return home by Ambassador, so G-ALZP was laid on for his return. Both George's and Churchill's return flights arrived at London at approximately the same time, with George able to savour the situation. In June 1953 he was invited to lunch by his old colleague Peter Masefield, who was now the boss of

BEA. He told George that the Ambassador was proving a real money earner, providing excellent service and its break-even load factor was working out at less than 50 per cent. Capt. Bailey of BEA asked George if he could find him a further six Ambassadors as the airline could do with them. George also commented that he had heard that Reg Butler of Butlers Air Transport regretted that the Ambassador was no longer available. He reportedly added that he was so impressed he wished he could get hold of the production jigs, ship them out to Australia and build the aircraft himself.

The reorganisation of the Christchurch factory, with many of the old faces having departed, meant there was no longer a need for a Chief Test Pilot. George was now just undertaking a few Vampire and Venom test flights so, in October 1953, being 'surplus to requirements', George was transferred to Hatfield to join the Comet's Technical Liaison team. On hearing this, George Miles wrote to George saying that if ever he was testing a Beaver, he should fly it down to Miles' airfield at Shoreham. George responded, 'I appreciate your invitation. When I feel bored with Hatfield, which will probably be on the second day, I shall come and see you.'

During his time with Airspeed, George had flown six prototypes – Oxford, Queen Wasp, Fleet Shadower, Horsa, Cambridge and Ambassador. He had flown 125 different types in approximately 5,200 test flights, totalling over 6,000 flying hours, the majority as pilot in charge. He considered it remarkable that no occupant of any of the test aircraft suffered an injury. George put this down to the outstanding work of the design, stress, workman, inspectors and flight crews. A farewell 'do' was held at the management club on 23 October where he said:

> Wherever I go the name of Airspeed will be held high and with dignity. You are saying goodbye to the old pilot who was too long suffering, too tolerant and perhaps too kind to rascals. You will be associating with a new pilot with new vision, new perspectives. This is a good thing and never compare the old pilot and old systems you are used to with the new pilot and systems you are not. To those who helped me so faithfully, patiently and who set a great example, it is never goodbye but au revoir.

Ambassador G-AKRD was flown to Dublin by George in January 1950 for demonstration to Aer Lingus, but no order materialised.

An embarrassing time for George on 13 March 1950 with G-AKRD sat on the runway at Hurn having failed to climb away following a single-engine take-off.

Again at Hurn and again George, this time G-ALFR after its right landing gear failed on landing on 12 July 1950, despite three green lights showing.

The Decca Navigation Mk 6 prototype receiver system, as tested by George in the Ambassador. He was full of praise for its accuracy.

Two autographed incidents – neither anything to do with George. Ron Clear's 'landing' of G-ALFR at Christchurch on 13 November 1950. He's signed the photo bottom right.

Brian Powell's incident with G-AMAD at Christchurch on 17 June 1951 – plus his signature. In both cases the aircraft were soon back in the air.

Seen at a quiet time, the Ambassador production line at Christchurch in 1950. A few years earlier it had been full of Horsas.

George in his office at Christchurch, surrounded by Christmas cards the various pilots had received.

Test pilots together. George (dark overalls) and John Cunningham admire G-ALFR at Hatfield, April 1951. Note the wording 'Elizabethan Class Prototype'.

Above and below: Also in 1951, G-ALZP visited Bristol Engines at Filton where George was able to compare its size with the resident Bristol Brabazon.

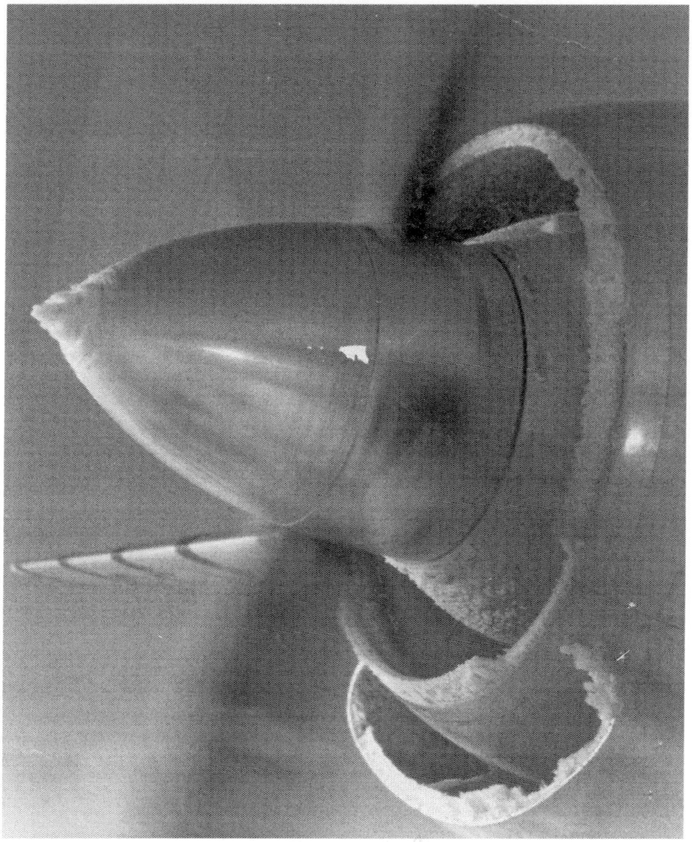

The later part of Ambassador testing included de-icing trials during 1951/52. Here ice has built up on the starboard engine nacelle.

De Havilland's takeover of Airspeed saw George involved in testing Vampire trainers at Christchurch during 1953.

Chapter 13

Family Life and Hobbies

There is little recorded with regard to George's personal life but, in spite of spending most of the war flying, he found time to become friendly with Lesley Kathleen Ziegler who lived at Hightown, Ringwood, close to Old Stacks. Her father was Major Colin Ziegler who was Commander of the Ringwood Home Guard. Lesley spent much of the war working at RAF Sopley Radar, frequently getting a lift in the CO's car as he lived in nearby Ibsley. Post-war she remained with the Royal Auxiliary Air Force at Sopley, also undertaking a secretarial course in London. George and Lesley were married on 16 September 1949 at Holy Trinity Church, Cookham, near Maidenhead. The ceremony was performed by the incumbent vicar – Revd Benjamin Hayward-Browne – who was married to George's sister. Press reports say that on leaving the church the newlyweds were saluted by John Cunningham who flew down in a Vampire. Rumour has it there were three aircraft involved and they turned up before the service ended. Due to their noise the verger was instructed to go outside and shoo them away! The noise level inside the church resulted in a panic attack by one gentleman who thought the London Blitz had returned. However, an elderly deaf lady slept through the whole event. George hired a Fairchild Argus from White Waltham for their honeymoon, stopping off for a few days in Dinard before reaching their destination of Lannion, in Brittany. After the honeymoon, George and Lesley set up home at Rockford End, just north of Ringwood, which was within easy travelling distance of Christchurch. The house was formerly part of the Somerley Estate, and included a large garden with a substantial wooded area, which was ideal for George's love of gardening. He would frequently take plant cuttings for his work colleagues at Christchurch. At the time George was still test flying Mosquitoes as well as the Ambassador. He would frequently fly low over Rockford End at the end of a flight as a signal to Lesley that he would be home in half an hour.

George's old friend Nevil contacted him in April 1948 to say he had bought a Proctor 5 with the intention of flying it to Australia and back with co-author James Riddle. As he had only flown a maximum of two hours at one stint, Nevil received further flying lessons on the Proctor from George at Portsmouth and Christchurch. Nevil and James set off from Eastleigh for Darwin on 22 September, starting their return flight early in 1949. Having got as far as Brindisi on 14 March, the Proctor suffered a ground loop, resulting in Nevil completing the final leg home by KLM. George and Lesley attended the Royal Aeronautical Society garden party at White Waltham on 8 May, meeting up with Nevil and Frances who updated them on the Proctor flight. Nevil and Frances emigrated to a farmstead near Melbourne in July 1950, with the Proctor following by sea in October.

George was awarded the OBE in the 1950 New Year's honours list in recognition of his flight test work. He became a Civil Officer of the OBE for his wartime flying of Mosquitoes and Spitfires, as well as for Airspeed. George's modesty meant that he didn't inform the directors of the honour – they only found out with the official announcement in the *London Gazette*. The Airspeed house magazine commented:

> Immensely enthusiastic, his experience and sound background of aeronautical engineering has put him in the top flight of test pilots. The good handling qualities of the Ambassador are due to Mr Errington's vigorous and intelligent approach to this serious business.

Prior to George's move to Hatfield, there were various events within the Errington household. In 1950 Lesley followed in her father's footsteps and became involved in local government, initially with Ringwood and Fordingbridge Rural District Council. George's father died in Oxford Hospital in October 1951 and was buried at Cookham Parish Cemetery along with his wife. That November saw the arrival of George and Lesley's first son – John. So, along with work, Lesley was kept busy whilst George was away. May 1953 saw the arrival of a daughter, Philippa, then in July 1955 a further son, Roland George.

Nevil called on the family in June 1953 whilst visiting England from his Melbourne home. He was researching for his next novel – *Requiem for a Wren*. In *Slide Rule*, published in 1954, Nevil described George as 'one of the best-known pilots in England'. Nevil sang the praises of Australian life but, at the time, George and his family were happy to stay in England.

George always had a passion for exotic cars. In 1935 he was driving a 12 hp Wolseley Dayton. Post-war he rebuilt a 1926 3 litre Bentley 'Old 3089' (RU 3089). Owned by a RAF officer during the war, George recovered it from a barn and slowly rebuilt it. It had been raced pre-war and George continued the tradition at Silverstone in 1949, wining his race. On a later visit to Exeter, George returned to the Bentley to find a policeman standing by it. Concerned as to what was amiss, George was surprised to find that the policeman was so in awe of the car that he wanted to meet its owner. After a short chat George drove away to a salute from the policeman. George always regarded Rockford End as home and had no intention of moving his family up to Hatfield, so he commuted in the Bentley, still calling in at the Christchurch factory. At times he wished he still had his own aircraft.

Just up George's street was the Goodwood Motor Circuit, which he visited on Easter Monday 1952. Grandstand seats had been arranged by de Havilland Engines, although George found the best part was his visit to the pits. He noted 'young Hawthorn is rising to stardom with a delightful velocity' – coming second in his Bristol-Cooper. George took part in racing at Ibsley Motor Racing Circuit, but not under his own name, but the pseudonym of Mr Gerrings. De Havilland objected to their Chief Test Pilot racing – hence the pseudonym. George was one of the more 'senior' drivers – he turned fifty in 1952. Ibsley had been a fighter station during the war and was close to Rockford End.

Meetings were arranged by the West Hants & Dorset Car Club, with the first race held on 4 August 1951. That year saw Colin Chapman race at Ibsley; 1952 saw Mike Hawthorn come first in a Bristol-Cooper. For the meeting on 18 April 1953 George raced his 500 cc Hybridus-JAP in the Formula III race. Bill Wootten was a flight engineer on the de Havilland flight test team, flying with George on Ambassador testing. They both shared an interest in motoring, Bill having worked for Cooper Racing Cars. George took him on as mechanic for his Hybridus, but Bill frequently complained to him that he took no notice of his advice for the engine set-up of the car.

Over the years George amassed a wide variety of other hobbies and interests. These included being a potential member of the 1927 English Ski Team. However, George had no time to train due to his other hobbies such as collecting and rebuilding old clocks (he owned many rare and valuable ones); exploring subterranean caves (including the Pennines and Africa); practising pianoforte to concert standard (he was a Chopin exponent); campanology; and cross-country walking and river fishing – including trips to Ireland with Nevil. On top of all this, the vast gardens at Rockford End were frequently open to the public, being renowned for their selection of flowering shrubs.

An Aeronautical garden party at White Waltham airfield in May 1949 – Nevil and his wife (left), Mrs Pike (from Hatfield), George and Lesley.

George and Lesley on their wedding day at Cookham on 16 September 1949. There were close family ties with the area.

The wedding cup presented to the newlyweds by the Ambassador Flight Crew at Christchurch.

George and Lesley set up home at Rockford End, just north of Ringwood. It was close to Moyles Court House, which was already well known to George.

George's great love – his 3 litre Bentley 'Old 3089' in which he covered many miles. He regularly commuted from Hatfield to home in the 1950s.

Seated in a visiting straight eight Bugatti 35 at Christchurch in the spring of 1952 – a famous race-winning type of the 1930s.

George's 500 cc Hybridus-JAP at Ibsley in April 1953. He knew the location well as it was just up the road from Rockford End.

A tight fit in the Hybridus-JAP, George on the starting line at Ibsley. He was one of the more 'senior' drivers.

Chapter 14

Hatfield Tasks and Vampire Travels

George arrived at de Havilland's main site at Hatfield in November 1953 as their customer liaison representative for sales of Comet 2 and 3 airliners. John Cunningham already had a large team of pilots at Hatfield, so there was little room for George. This was despite the Ministry of Supply having written to de Havilland stating that 'approval is given for G. B. S. Errington to carry out test flights and ferrying of all types of de Havilland Aircraft'. However, George soon 'lost' his new job following the Comet 1 fatal crashes in the spring of 1954. The airliner was grounded, as was the Comet 2, so there were no aircraft for George to sell. Not an encouraging start.

As well as the Comet, Hatfield was involved in military aircraft. It was building Vampire Trainers and Venoms for the RAF, Sea Venoms for the Royal Navy, plus Vampire fighters for export. As George had experience of flying Vampire Trainers at Christchurch, it was agreed that he would assist the Hatfield team with these aircraft. One of George's first tasks (prior to the Comet grounding) concerned Vampire T55s for the Chilean Air Force. Five had been ordered and flown at Hatfield during the winter of 1953/54. They were shipped to Santiago, whence George was dispatched to supervise their assembly and test flying. Assembled at El Cerrillos airport, the first was ready for test flying on 28 April, being flown by a Chilean Wing Commander the following day. George remained until the end of June to oversee the test flying of all five aircraft, prior to handover. One was lost in September when the aircraft entered a spin from which it failed to recover. However, George's memory of Chile was of the charm of the country with its delightful exasperatingly irresponsible people.

In the summer of 1954 George was contacted by George Miles from Shoreham. A pre-war Miles Sparrowhawk had been rebuilt as a racer with two small Turbomeca Palas jet engines. Now known as the Sparrowjet, a number of races had been completed by racing ace Fred Dunkerley, but there appeared to be lack of power from the engines. George Miles had tried various fixes unsuccessfully and called upon his old colleague for his experience and help. George visited Shoreham on 25 October to test fly the Sparrowjet. However, he was unable to increase the Sparrowjet's top speed or come up with an answer to the problem. Eventually the problem was solved, and the aircraft achieved 228 mph in the 1957 Kings Cup Race.

The Burmese Air Force ordered eight Vampire Trainers in September 1954 (it already operated Venom FB50s). The first four departed Hatfield on 7 December en route to Mingaladon Air Base, near Rangoon. George oversaw the flight, with three pilots from Airwork flying the other aircraft. On arrival at Mingaladon George undertook a demonstration flight for the Air Force Brass, which involved emitting smoke, something that hadn't been seen before over Rangoon. Traffic came to a standstill and George's display was a talking point for days. It was then down to the mundane task of training local pilots onto the jet. Two of the first pilots converted were Ko Gyi and Maung Maung Nyunt, who later became Lt Colonels. They wrote:

> George was our teacher as well as our friend and from the beginning he drove our nervousness out of us by his brilliant demonstration and masterful handling. In his hands the aircraft was like a Tiger Moth and it was our great fortune that we were introduced to jet flying by such a wonderful aviator.

4 January 1955 was Burma's Independence Day, which saw a fly-past of the new jet squadron. However, their senior pilot proved incapable of flying, so George was secreted within the lead Vampire to head the Independence Day fly-past commemorating the kicking out of the British! The other four Vampires departed Hatfield in February 1955 on delivery, with George briefly overseeing their entry into service. George had time to visit Rangoon and its Golden Pagoda before returning home in early March.

Having developed the Dove and Heron airliners at Hatfield, de Havilland undertook their production at Chester with Geoffrey Pike, one of the senior test pilots. At the beginning of 1955 a Heron 2 undertook a sales tour of South America, with George involved as demonstration pilot. At the end of the tour the Heron did not return home but was sold in July to Bahamas Airways. George was responsible for its official handover at Nassau in August, taking over from the airline's fleet of Grumman Goose amphibians.

Eight Vampire Trainers were purchased by the Indonesian Air Force in 1955 and test flown at Hatfield during that autumn. They were then packed for dispatch by sea to Djakarta. Once again, George was head of the team that sailed to Djakarta to oversee their re-assembly and test flying. The Vampires were taken to Hussein Air Base, Bandung, for assembly by an Indonesian team under the watchful eye of George. The first was successfully flown on 18 January 1956, ending with an aerobatic display for which the ATC controller had instructed George 'to go to it as they would keep everyone else away'. At the time there were only two Indonesian Air Force jet pilots. Having been trained by the RAF at Little Rissington, they would be in charge of training the next four pilots. Six of the Vampires were officially handed over on 20 February with George again giving an aerobatic display. During the flight George carried a reporter from the local radio station who gave a live commentary of the event. Word of the 'Jet Professor' spread around Bandung, which resulted in the event getting out of hand. On landing, the locals burst through the police lines, swarmed around the aircraft and then rushed towards George as he taxied in. George managed one more flight during the afternoon, taking a quick trip to Djakarta in just over eight minutes. The local press commented on George's 'uniform' – bow tie, shirt sleeves and tropical helmet – which was in complete contrast to American pilots. During his stay, George gave flights to the editors of two local newspapers in order to impress them with the new British jet. This did not work quite as George anticipated, being asked 'why was an English pilot flying an American plane'? George pointed out the Vampire was not an American plane. 'Yes, it must be – the English don't make jet aeroplanes.' You can't win them all! George and the de Havilland team departed Bandung by train for Djakarta. There they boarded a Garuda Convair 340 for Singapore, where George switched to a Cathay Pacific DC-6 and flew on to Hong Kong. Here George was greeted by Bill Dudman, as he had been back in 1937. That evening a few drinks were taken to help recall past memories! George then set off for Tokyo and his next sales pitch.

The Japanese Air Self Defence Force also indicated their interest in the Vampire Trainer and ordered one in 1955 for evaluation. This was delivered by sea to Hamamatsu Air Base early in 1956, and George was selected to demonstrate it to the 'Brass'. On arrival in Tokyo he found his reputation had preceded him, with the press out in numbers to greet the 'Jet Professor'. Due to his being an English pilot in Japan, the event again attracted local radio coverage. The runway at Hamamatsu was being resurfaced and the visiting 'Brass' were unable to land there, travelling by road the 200 miles from Tokyo. George was not deterred and undertook over 100 take-offs and landings on the half of the runway still available. Despite requiring additional braking, the Vampire survived with its original set of tyres. The 'Brass' commented that a visiting Lockheed T-33 needed to replace its tyres every twenty landings. Another boost for the British! After flight testing, the Vampire was officially handed over on the 9 March. Then followed familiarisation flights with Air Force officers, which enabled George to take in the beauty of the Japanese Alps and Mount Fuji at close hand. George demonstrated the Vampire's inverted flying capability to a General. He flew down to ground level, inverted the Vampire, climbed away to 6,000 feet and returned for the final circuit – still upside down. The local journalists asked why he flew upside down, to which George replied:

> Japan is a beautiful country and just now the cherry blossoms are at their best. It's a lot easier to see the blossoms that way.

A few days later George was summoned to the hangar, where he found the Vampire sitting on its belly. It had been lowered off its trestle without the undercarriage being fixed 'down', hence an ominous crunch was heard as the wheels folded up and the Vampire hit the deck. It was soon repaired to enable George to continue his demonstrations – his last was on 14 April. He remained in Tokyo, sightseeing for a few days, before returning home via Rangoon. His best memory was of an air force officer who commented after his flight, 'Yes, magnificent. I always knew the English made good aeroplanes.' George reported back to Hatfield that the Vampire had done wonders and brought much credit to de Havilland and to England. Unfortunately, the Japanese already had Lockheed T-33s trainers on order and so did not proceed with a Vampire order.

In conjunction with BEA, de Havilland's PR department issued press releases in the mid-1950s on the Ambassador's in-service performance. These reported the fine record of BEA's Elizabethans, which showed the highest load factor in their fleet. However, the reports were not well received by George as they referred to the 'de Havilland Ambassador'. Eventually BEA decided to expand its turbo-prop Viscount fleet and by 1957 had received sufficient numbers to enable some of their Ambassadors to be withdrawn. In June, three were sold to Butlers Air Transport of Sydney for £450,000. With George's experience, he was asked by BEA to lead their team of pilots and engineers in flying the aircraft out to Sydney the following month. The de Havilland directors agreed, with Ron Clear joining George as one of the other pilots. Departing Heathrow, the aircraft headed south-eastwards for the long flight to Australia, making landfall at Darwin. George commented that the flight was much easier than his trip to Hong Kong and China in the summer of 1937. The three Ambassadors eventually arrived in formation over Sydney Harbour on 18 June, before being handed over to the directors of Butlers. There was again a sense of déjà vu for George as he had previously demonstrated the Ambassador to them in England in 1950. Whilst at Sydney Airport on 17 July, he was overjoyed to meet up with Nevil Norway again. Nevil happened to be flying out of Sydney with his wife by Qantas, en route to a holiday in Fiji. George, Ron and the BEA crews then flew home by BOAC.

George was now regarded as a de Havilland demonstration pilot which saw him return to South America with their Vampire trainer demonstrator. Flown at Chester in October 1956, it was shipped to Buenos Aires for the start of a sales tour, with George supervising its reassembly at Moron Air Base. He tested the Vampire on 15 December prior to setting off on an extensive tour taking in Argentina, Peru and Uruguay before ending in Chile the following April.

The first demonstrations were to the Argentine Air Force and Navy at Aeroparque Airport on 21 December. Further demonstrations followed until moving on to the Naval Base of Espora on 22 January 1957, then to the easterly Naval Base of Punta del Indio, where George was concerned to find the runway composed of crushed seashells and loose stones. He didn't consider this suitable for take-off, so arranged for the Vampire to be towed to an adjacent airfield that was under construction. George returned to Moron prior to the next stage, which involved the first non-stop crossing of the Andes by a single-engined jet. No pressure then! He later found out that a Chipmunk had made the flight from Argentina to Santiago in October 1954 – so a bit of a let-down. Take-off was made with full tanks, then a climb to height before crossing the Andes at 35,000 feet towards Chile, followed by a decent to El Cerrillos. Here George met up again with Air Force officials he had met on his previous visit in 1954. The next stop was Peru and, concerned at the changeable weather ahead, George built in a fuel stop at the Chilean airfield at Arica. However, the airfield was still under construction and he had to land on the perimeter track, luckily without any problems. The Air Force had laid on refuelling facilities – drums of fuel pumped by a hand pump!

On to Lima with thunderstorms over the Andes to the east, and stratus cloud covering the Pacific to the west. Demonstrations for the Peruvian Air Force were undertaken – they were about to receive Hunter fighters from Britain. George returned to Chile on 14 February and wanted to omit the fuel stop at Arica, but a direct route to Antofagasta meant a long stretch over the Pacific. After studying the weather reports, George opted for the direct flight. As anticipated, the first 200 miles were in cloud, but then the Pacific appeared below. With 600 miles flown, George was relieved to pick up the Antofagasta radio beacon. After a brief stop it was off on a further 700 miles to Santiago for demonstrations to the Chileans. As in Japan, George found he was following the demonstration of a Lockheed T-33 by the Americans. After a few days it was across the Andes again, this time destination Montevideo, for demonstration to Uruguay Air Force and Navy 'Brass'. George also gave a flight to the British Ambassador whom he described as the most interesting and informed passenger of the whole tour. On 7 March it was back to Buenos Aires to take part in a 'navigational exercise' taking in Moron and Cordoba, which was only a grass airfield. Gunnery trials at Moron resulted in clods of earth striking the starboard wing, but with little damage. George then had an appointment in Montevideo to take part in the Santos Dumas aviation celebrations. George found that none of the South Americans he spoke to had heard of the Wright Brothers – in their eyes, the Brazilian, Dumas, was the pioneer of aviation. George departed Argentina on 16 April and headed across the Andes for Santiago once again. He ran into an unexpected weather front, which meant crossing half of the Andes on instruments alone, with a 65 knot headwind necessitating a constant eye on the dwindling fuel level. At Santiago his Air Force contacts informed him they had agreed to purchase the Vampire to replace the one that had crashed earlier. The only other sale resulting from the tour was of five Vampires to Venezuela in 1958. George summed up:

> The little Vampire with its Goblin jet had functioned perfectly and I had not a moment's uneasiness on that account in five months' flying. It had certainly been a very interesting 30,000 miles.

George also recalled the vast and fertile plains of Argentina, the sinister deserts of West Peru and its Inca traditions in the Eastern areas, and the volcanoes of the vast Cordillera which few had seen. He departed Santiago for Lima, where the Peruvian Air Force was interested in purchasing twenty Vampires but had no money. It was then on to Mexico and Toronto en route home.

With his move to de Havilland at Hatfield in 1953, George expected to be involved with Comets. Instead, he became their Vampire trainer demonstration pilot.

George overseeing the delivery of eight Vampire trainers to the Burmese Air Force at Mingaladon Air Base, December 1954.

For a change, George demonstrated a Heron 2 around South America before handing it over to Bahamas Airways at their Nassau base in August 1955.

In the spring of 1956 George visited Japan to demonstrate Vampire trainer 63-5571 to the Japanese Defence Force.

George (seated, second left) poses for a group photo with Japanese officials and pilots in front of the Vampire.

On their sale to Butlers Air Transport, George was requested to fly one of three former BEA Ambassadors out to Sydney in June 1957.

George's trademark 'flying suit' whilst demonstrating the Vampire trainer. Jacket and spotted red bow tie. The 1950s were a different era!

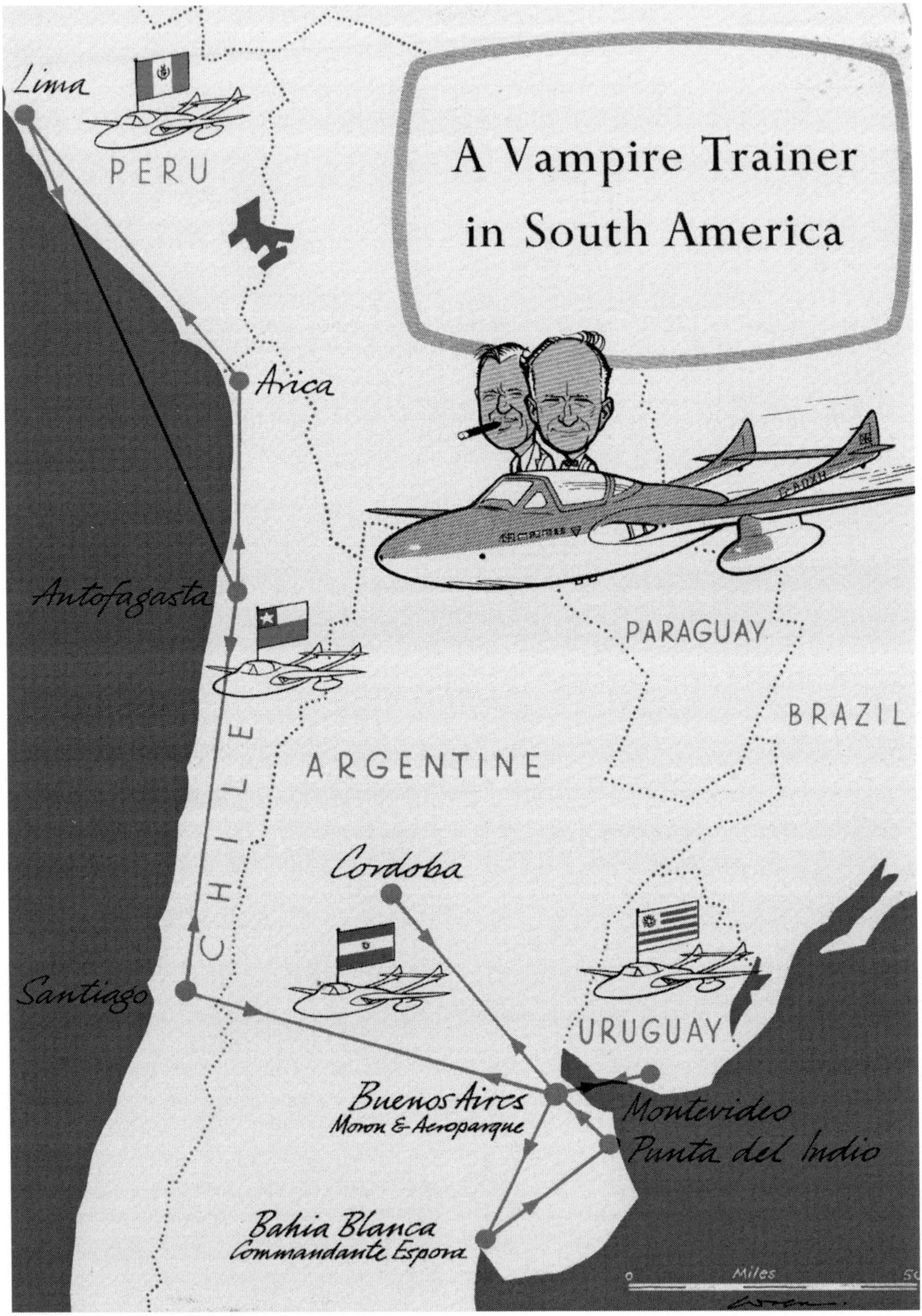

De Havilland issued this publicity map in connection with George's South American tour in early 1957.

Chapter 15

Ending with Big Jets

De Havilland undertook the extensive modification of a number of Comet 2s for use by the RAF. These were delivered to 216 Sqd at Lyneham, from June 1956, with George overseeing their entry into service, travelling on many of their long-range flights. Comet 4 test flying commenced at Hatfield in the spring of 1958, but there was no place for George on the test pilot team. This was led by John Cunningham with production test flying in charge of Pat Fillingham. However, George was involved in a number of demonstration and delivery flights.

The first production Comet 4 was flown by John Cunningham on the evening of 27 April 1958 and flew a number of proving flights towards being awarded its C of A. It flew to Hong Kong for the opening of the airport's new runway on 12 September. Then, on 16 September, it undertook a promotional flight to North and South America, with George as part of the team. Also on board were BOAC crews for training, prior to the Comet entering service. The first stage of the tour was to Gander, which enabled George to recall his Constellation flight ten years earlier. How speed and noise levels had changed in those few years. Next was Montreal, then Toronto and Ottawa, before crossing to Vancouver on 22 September for further airline demonstrations, including Canadian Pacific. There was a brief respite before heading south to Mexico City's airport at 7,340 feet above sea level – a good test for any airliner. After demonstrations to Mexicana, the Comet departed at full load for Lima and was easily airborne despite there being no wind. This was down to the power of the four Avon engines and the generous area of flaps provided on the Comet. Again, George recalled the progress since he had promoted flaps on the Envoy back in 1935. Demonstrations at Lima again confirmed that the Comet did not need a long runway for take-offs, even at high load. It was then east across the Andes to Buenos Aires, where Aerolineas Argentinas had ordered six Comets in March and the airline was keen to see its performance. Rio de Janeiro and Caracas were visited before a long leg back up to New York, then home to Hatfield on 27 September, the team having covered 23,000 miles. From George's point of view, this had been luxury travel compared with what he had undertaken in previous years. Two days later the Comet was awarded its C of A and it entered service with BOAC on the New York route on 4 October.

The first Aerolineas Argentinas aircraft departed on delivery on 2 March 1959, piloted by John Cunningham with George among the crew, taking eighteen and a half hours for the 7,075-mile flight. Initially, George was concerned about the state of Aerolineas

Argentinas' fleet when he spied an ancient Latécoère 26 airliner parked at Buenos Aires. However, this had been pulled out of a museum especially for the event. Their second Comet flew out from Hatfield a few days later to enable the airline to commence services on 16 April. Along with Peter Wilson, George remained in Buenos Aires in order to train additional crews. At one of the remote airfields visited, the crew had to wait for locals to clear the runway before they could take-off. George was not happy to learn that the third Comet, delivered on 2 May, only lasted a few weeks as it crashed on approach to Asunción, Paraguay, on 27 August and was damaged beyond repair.

The Dove continued to be a best-seller for de Havilland, with the improved Dove 8 introduced in 1960. George was involved as customer liaison, with an early sale made to JCB Excavators. Their Dove was delivered in December 1960 and George undertook some flights with JCB's Capt. Sutton the following summer. This included a 1,400-mile trip to various JCB factories around Europe with the Dove making use of local airfields, not inconvenient airports. This backed up George's long-held view that if you had an aircraft you had to make full use of it to get you where you wanted to go – not some distant airport. It demonstrated the correct use of an aircraft as a business tool – something he had realised with his Swift back in the mid-1930s.

George was an advocate for improving navigation aids for pilots, the need increasing with the introduction of jet travel in the late 1950s. Decca developed a navigation system that reached a highly sophisticated form for airways navigation by the mid-1960s, and George was a strong supporter of it. He had seen its practical use in his trip in the JCB Dove. George had got to know the Decca bosses in his capacity as a test pilot. In 1963 the company needed to replace its Valetta trials aircraft and George came up with the answer. He knew the King of Morocco had a VIP Ambassador for sale and that it would suit Decca's needs. The deal was agreed, and the Decca pilots flew out to Rabat, along with George. He negotiated a bargain sale price of £3,000 and arranged to fly the aircraft back to Gatwick. Here it received attention from Air Couriers before entering service with Decca. Amongst its trial and demonstration flight was one across the North Atlantic to New York, in September 1964. This was something that even George had not achieved and is believed to be the only visit of an Ambassador to North America. George recalled how he had flown the Ambassador prototype with an early form of Decca Navigation back in 1950.

With George away from home so much, plus Lesley involved in local government and many local committees, it was decided to send the children away to boarding schools. In the late 1950s, John went to Radley College, Abingdon, and, later, Roly to St Leonards-on-Sea. George settled into a routine of staying near Hatfield during the week, returning to Rockford at weekends. This gave him the opportunity to visit family and friends around the Hertfordshire area. George was saddened to learn of Nevil's death at his home in Melbourne in January 1960. After a while his widow Frances returned to live on the Suffolk coast, confirming that Nevil always had a high regard for George.

In January 1960 de Havilland became part of Hawker Siddeley Aviation, resulting in a malaise seeming to settle over Hatfield. In August 1961 George heard that Hawker

Siddeley had put the Portsmouth site up for sale. On top of this, in November it was announced that the Christchurch site was to be closed by July 1962. The loss of his former 'homes' did nothing to help George's feelings towards Hatfield. During the 1960s he became responsible for operations liaison with airlines flying Comets and Tridents. He also helped as required on test work for Hawker Siddeley, which enabled him to undertake occasional test flying of Comet 4s and Trident 1s. The Trident had been first flown by John Cunningham in January 1962. John took on additional test pilots for Trident development work but, again, George was not included. The first Tridents were delivered to BEA early in 1964 and George flew a number of the subsequent aircraft at Hatfield prior to delivery. At the Farnborough show in September 1964, George was part of the Trident crew, probably having been asked along by Ron Clear. On one of the show days George took along young Roly. He recalls that he was introduced to the other pilots but, as he recounts in the Foreword, whilst the Trident was being demonstrated, he was left to sit on the grass outside the pilot's tent.

Hawker Siddeley became involved with the Riley Dove in 1965/66. The original DH Dove had been updated by Riley Aircraft in the United States and it was planned that conversions would be undertaken by McAlpine Aviation at Luton. George was in favour of the plan and undertook test flying one of the converted aircraft at Cambridge, early in 1966. There was talk of Hawker Siddeley building new airframes to supply to the conversion line. Unfortunately, there were problems in obtaining UK certification for the modified aircraft and the project was abandoned in the UK.

George was going to turn sixty-five in January 1967. So, although dreading it, he started planning for retirement, possibly as early as August 1966, when he anticipated being able to spend time in the garden, go fishing and sailing. But none of this was to be. On 15 April 1966 George attended the first Airspeed reunion dinner at the Chewton Glen Hotel in Highcliffe, reacquainting himself with many former colleagues. The 21 May saw a garden party and flying display at Booker, where George caught up with Sir Alan Cobham before flying one of the old timers. Then at Hatfield on the late afternoon of 3 June he accompanied Peter Barlow as co-pilot on the first flight of Trident G-ARPY in order to obtain its C of A, prior to delivery to BEA. During the course of the flight the aircraft undertook a number of stall tests – something that had been done many times. With its C of G well aft, the Trident entered a super stall from which it could not recover. Despite full power being applied to the three Speys, the aircraft entered a flat spin from 10,000 feet before hitting the ground like a brick at Felthorpe, near Norwich, at 18.35. Both pilots and the two test observers were killed outright. George had not been scheduled to fly that day, standing in at the last moment as the pilot due to accompany Peter was unavailable. The CAA report concluded that the pilot had delayed positive recovery actions by a few seconds too long, making recovery from the stall impossible.

A tragic event ended George's thirty years of test flying for Airspeed, de Havilland and Hawker Siddeley, during which he amassed 6,800 flying hours. His funeral was held on 9 June at Ellingham Church, close to his Rockford home, with large numbers of his former pilot colleagues attending. This was followed by a private family cremation.

In March 1959 there was a large turnout at Buenos Aires to see the arrival of Aerolineas Argentinas' first Comet 4 LV-PLM. George is probably in there somewhere.

George backed the Dove 8 as a business tool for getting from A to B quickly, just as he had done with his Swift in the 1930s.

Trident 1 G-ARPB was demonstrated at the September 1964 Farnborough Air Show with George on board for the ride.

On the evening of 3 June 1966 we see the smouldering remains of Trident G-ARPY in the field at Felthorpe. On stalling, it had spun out of the sky, dropping like a brick.

Chapter 16

A Fitting Tribute

Following George's death, the family received many tributes from family and friends around the world, many of whom were unknown to Lesley. One theme was how they enjoyed the times George visited them. The following extracts paint a picture of George's character as seen by his colleagues:

A great pilot and a very fine man – Sir Alan Cobham
I have flown many enjoyable hours with George. He lived a very full life – Hessell Tiltman
A remarkable man in many ways – Arthur Hagg
A character of rare quality in a drab world – George Miles
The aviation world is poorer for his passing – Decca Navigation

George had always maintained close contact with the press and been happy to give them information and articles on his work with Airspeed. In his latter days at Christchurch he became a close friend of Brian Mead – the Editor of the *Christchurch Times*. This is an extract of Brian's tribute:

> In four decades George Errington flew most kinds of aircraft through practically every sort of experience in almost all the countries there are. At the age of 64, and some four months prior to retiring, sitting as second pilot in what is one of the safest aeroplanes in the world, on a summer evening over Norfolk, he died. Had George Errington survived the crash the experience would have been added to his unending fund of stories to be related with dry relish. One can hear him saying '—and there we were — quite definitely running out of sky — in a big way'.
>
> Although G. B. S. Errington had done so much, no one could have been more modest. He did such extraordinary things. Like delivering an aircraft to China or being the first man to fly the east-west crossing of South America in a single engined jet, or running a vintage Bentley which he refused to disfigure by displaying the road licence which, of course, he bought.
>
> His quiet, measured, detached mien may have done more than any other individual to embellish the English reputation abroad and the good name of British aircraft. Whether he was delivering Envoys or testing Spitfires or towing Horsas or demonstrating Vampires or flying Comets or helping to develop the Decca Flight Log or relaxing in

his beloved Ambassador, George Errington contributed in a big way to achieving that supremacy for Britain. It could never be said that in his flying he became part of the machine. Rather one should say that the machine became part of him.

There is a difference!'

Lesley and the children remained at Rockford End. Lesley continued her local government work, progressing to a Hampshire County Councillor in 1974 and Chairman of the New Forest District Council in 1977/78. She stood down from these duties in the early '90s, although still supporting many local societies. Lesley died on 22 June 1998. Rockford End remained in the family with George's son Roly continuing to look after the house and gardens in the manner his father would have appreciated.

Following the sale by Hawker Siddeley of some of the Hatfield airfield site for housing, the developers used appropriate names for many of the roads. Errington Close can be found in the Garden Village adjacent to Mosquito Way, along with the likes of Cunningham Avenue and Barlow Close. From an aviation point of view, George's name is recorded, along with many of his contemporaries, in the Test Pilots' Memorial Roll of Honour, held at the FAST Museum, Farnborough, a fitting place to be remembered.

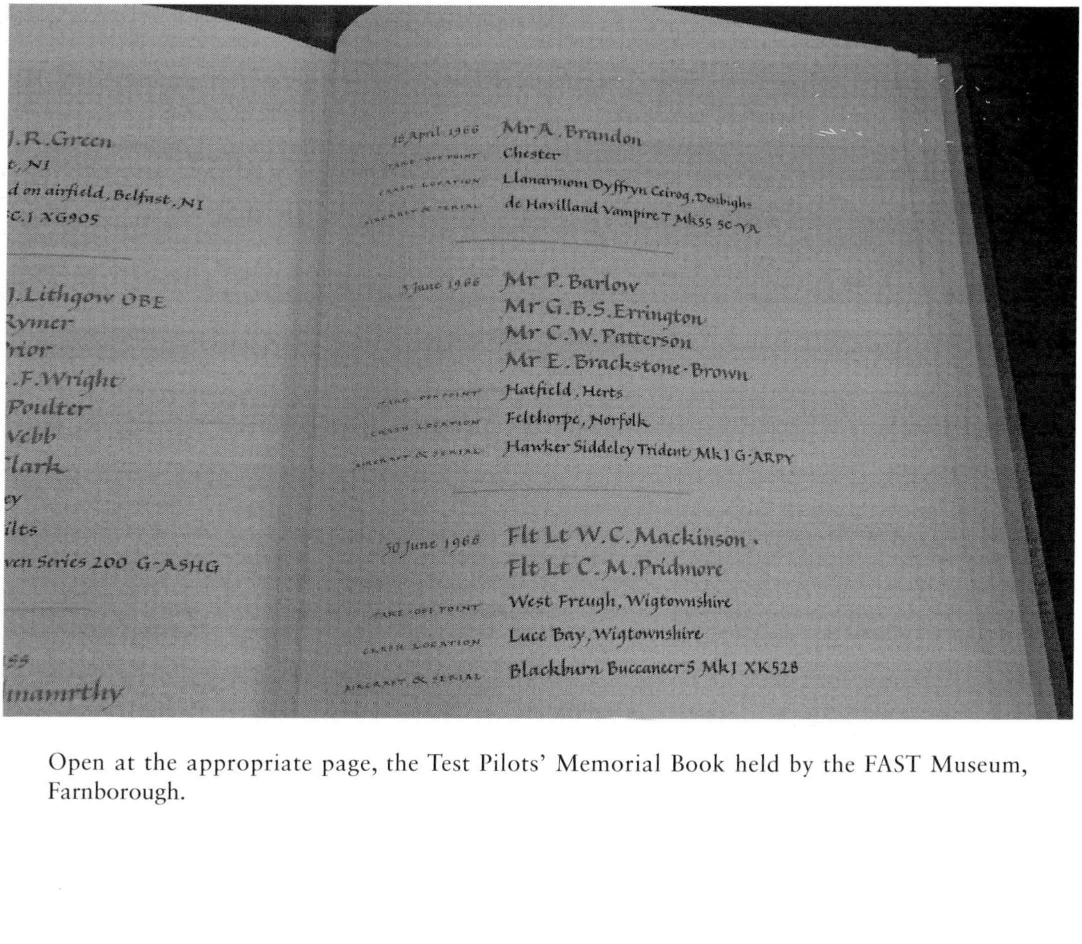

Open at the appropriate page, the Test Pilots' Memorial Book held by the FAST Museum, Farnborough.

Still looking dapper – George at Farnborough in the early 1960s.